The Psychoanalytic Encounter and the Misuse of Theory

In clear, accessible language, Lee Grossman addresses the disjuncture between analytic literature and clinical work in an effort to render analytic theorizing more representative of clinical experience.

Pointing out the ways in which analytic literature can fail to capture the intensity of feeling and the stumbling, lurching, working in the dark that captures much of clinical engagement, Grossman shows how incomprehensibility is sometimes mistaken for wisdom. As an alternative, Grossman shows how attention to what he calls the syntax of thought can naturally define three different broad categories of life experience: the omnipotence of the neurotic, the wishful, short-sighted thinking of the perverse, and the concrete, disordered thinking of the psychotic. Using rich clinical material, interspersed with detailed exposition and artful satire, Grossman departs from conventional theoretical writing to provide new ways of conceptualizing analytic therapy.

Addressing analytic therapy as an encounter between two people, both governed by forces about which they know very little, this book provides essential insights for psychoanalysts, psychotherapists, and other clinical practitioners both in training and in practice.

Lee Grossman is a training and supervising analyst at the San Francisco Center for Psychoanalysis and a member of the editorial board of the *Journal of the American Psychoanalytic Association*. He served on the editorial board of *The Psychoanalytic Quarterly* for 15 years. He lives in Oakland with his analyst wife, Jan Baeuerlen, and a goofy English bulldog named Frank.

The Psychoanalytic Encounter and the Misuse of Theory

Lee Grossman

Routledge
Taylor & Francis Group

LONDON AND NEW YORK

Designed cover image: 'Theory and Practice' by Lee Grossman

First published 2023
by Routledge
4 Park Square, Milton Park, Abingdon, Oxon OX14 4RN

and by Routledge
605 Third Avenue, New York, NY 10158

Routledge is an imprint of the Taylor & Francis Group, an informa business

British Library Cataloguing-in-Publication Data
A catalogue record for this book is available from the British Library

ISBN: 9781032419237 (hbk)
ISBN: 9781032419244 (pbk)
ISBN: 9781003360391 (ebk)

DOI: 10.4324/9781003360391

Typeset in Garamond
by Newgen Publishing UK

For Jan
where all the ladders start

Contents

Acknowledgments

I once had a patient who knew that his analysis was a training case. He suggested that I pay him for the education. I didn't, but I am grateful. Everyone says it, but it is nonetheless true: My patients and my students are the teachers to whom I owe the most.

My introduction to analytic thought came from my father, Carl M. Grossman. My introduction to writing came from my mother, Sylva Grossman, whom I also blame for my sense of humor. It was from her that I learned that some wisecracks are obligatory in certain situations.

The first time I discussed a paper in public, it was Warren Poland's "Insight and the Analytic Dyad." I was an analytic candidate, so I still knew everything. Despite my complete failure to understand the paper's wisdom, I criticized it line by line. Warren responded by saying it was the first time he was sure a discussant had actually read his paper. In the years since, he has become a generous colleague, a trusted advisor, and a dear friend. I suspect that all who know Warren think of him as their best friend.

My first study group was in the form of regular walks with Jim Dimon when we were candidates. I owe special thanks to Louis Roussel and Janis Baeuerlen, with whom I have a study group that continues to this day. Louis has been a valued colleague and teaching partner for many years. Jan, to whom I have been married since medical school, has forborne to read every word I have written, in some cases through countless drafts. And yet we are still together. Her perspective as a child analyst, along with my unofficial participation in the child analytic group at the San Francisco Center for Psychoanalysis, has been a tonic for my clinical work and a physic for my pomp.

I had the good fortune to do my psychiatric residency at Mount Zion Hospital in San Francisco, a program run by gifted analysts and psychodynamic therapists, across the street from the analytic institute. My residency overlapped the beginning of my analytic training, and the transition was seamless. At Mount Zion Shirley Cooper, the best therapist I have ever met, showed me how to listen from the heart and instilled in me a respect for child work bordering on awe, which continues to this day. Erik Erikson and Otto Will ran a seminar that made an impact on me far greater than its brief duration would suggest. Above all, they helped me learn from my patients. Erik Gann and Phyllis Cath brought analytic ideas to life. Phillip Spielman taught me how to stop and smell the analytic roses, and Owen Renik taught me how to cut to the chase. My debt to Owen is evidenced by the frequency of my references to his work throughout the text.

The work of Victor Calef and Edward Weinshel, along with Jacob Arlow, got me interested in the uses of negation and disavowal. Arlow read and encouraged me with my first paper.

When I was still a medical student doing a psychiatry rotation, I had a tutorial with Thomas Ogden, with whom I did a close reading of Brenner's *Elementary Textbook of Psychoanalysis.* It was a masterclass in reading analytic theory.

My major theoretical debt after Freud is to Hans Loewald, who reconciled and recast Freud's thinking in a way that made sense of developmental processes, made room for spirituality and growth, gave the social world its due, reformulated "drives" and "object relations," and introduced a note of optimism absent in Freud.

As an undergraduate in philosophy, I studied existentialism and phenomenology with Maurice Natanson, a philosopher who had a profound respect for psychoanalysis. Gregory Bateson's thinking about thinking and Alan Watts's Tao-flavored Buddhism also influenced me deeply.

There are too many other professional influences throughout my career to list them all, but I would like to mention Dale Boesky, Merton Gill, and especially Lawrence Friedman, who introduced me to the idea of looking at the psychological function of theorizing.

I would like to thank my first analyst, Ernest J. White, for saving my life, and my wife, Janis Baeuerlen, for making it worth living. Thanks also to Mitchell Wilson, whose critique led me to change my title, and to Kate Hawes, Georgina Clutterbuck, and the team at Routledge, who reined in my excesses and turned this into a book.

Special thanks are due to Daphne de Marneffe and Louis Roussel for their careful reading and commentary on earlier drafts. I have incorporated many of their ideas in the final draft. The fault for all remaining inadequacies is mine alone.

I am grateful to the following psychoanalytic journals for allowing me to reprint material in modified form that originally appeared in their pages:

fort da

"Neurosis as a way of thinking: The syntax of unconscious oedipal mentation" (2018), 24, 57–65.
"In and out of the frame: Moving between fantasy and reality in movies and psychoanalysis" (2006), 12, 8–17.

The International Journal of Psychoanalysis

" 'Psychic reality' and reality testing in the analysis of perverse defences" (1996), 77, 509–17. © Institute of Psycho-Analysis, London, 1996. Wiley.

The Psychoanalytic Quarterly

"The person in the analyst's chair: A dialogue with Abend's 'Countertransference and psychoanalytic technique' " (2018), 87, 517–32. © The Psychoanalytic Quarterly, reprinted by permission of Taylor & Francis Ltd, www.tandfonline.com, on behalf of The Psychoanalytic Quarterly.

"Reading Ogden Reading Winnicott" (2017), 86, 693–98. © The Psychoanalytic Quarterly, reprinted by permission of Taylor & Francis Ltd, www.tandfonline.com, on behalf of The Psychoanalytic Quarterly.

"The syntax of oedipal thought in the case of Little Hans" (2015), 84, 469–78. © The Psychoanalytic Quarterly, reprinted by permission of Taylor & Francis Ltd, www.tandfonline.com, on behalf of The Psychoanalytic Quarterly.

"The object-preserving function of sadomasochism" (2015), 84, 643–64. © The Psychoanalytic Quarterly, reprinted by permission of Taylor & Francis Ltd, www.tandfonline.com, on behalf of The Psychoanalytic Quarterly.

"Inventing oneself: A note on the effort toward self-cure in a psychotic woman" (2014), 83, 681–90. © The Psychoanalytic Quarterly, reprinted by permission of Taylor & Francis Ltd, www.tandfonline.com, on behalf of The Psychoanalytic Quarterly.

"The third wish: Some thoughts on using magic against magic" (2013), 82, 477–82. © The Psychoanalytic Quarterly, reprinted by permission of Taylor & Francis Ltd, www.tandfonline.com, on behalf of The Psychoanalytic Quarterly.

"What the analyst does not hear" (1999), 68, 84–98. © The Psychoanalytic Quarterly, reprinted by permission of Taylor & Francis Ltd, www.tandfonline.com, on behalf of The Psychoanalytic Quarterly.

"A note on empathy and the analyst's transference" (1996), 65, 372–5. © The Psychoanalytic Quarterly, reprinted by permission of Taylor & Francis Ltd, www.tandfonline.com, on behalf of The Psychoanalytic Quarterly.

"The analyst's influence" (1996), 65, 681–92. © The Psychoanalytic Quarterly, reprinted by permission of Taylor & Francis Ltd, www.tandfonline.com, on behalf of The Psychoanalytic Quarterly.

"The perverse attitude toward reality" (1993), 62, 422–36. © The Psychoanalytic Quarterly, reprinted by permission of Taylor & Francis Ltd, www.tandfonline.com, on behalf of The Psychoanalytic Quarterly.

The Psychoanalytic Review

"Psychoanalytic technique: A reconsideration of the concept" (2014), 101, 431–49.

The San Francisco Center for Psychoanalysis Newsletter

"The duration of analysis. A contribution to the discussion" (2007), September, p. 4.

Introduction

What Is This, Who Am I, and Why Should You Care?

Psychoanalysis is divided. The confusion of theoretical tongues is recognized and bemoaned by many analysts, although some see it as a good sign for future growth. But there is a more fundamental division that, for the most part, goes unremarked: Analytic teaching and writing are increasingly disconnected from clinical experience. Instead, increasingly arcane theories are deflecting attention from the passions and terrors of clinical engagement.

This is a book about the psychoanalytic encounter — how it is lived by the participants and how it is unintentionally misrepresented by the analytic literature. It is a response to three impressions I have had in my 40 years as an analytic clinician, consultant, teacher, writer, and editor. They are:

1. Psychoanalytic therapy is hard. Unnecessary theoretical complexity makes it harder.
2. The theories that analysts espouse in the literature bear only a slight connection to the way they actually work.
3. Educators and researchers often discuss analysis as if it were a reproducible treatment.

Analysis is hard because the therapist's mind obeys the same psychological rules as the patient's. Both patient and analyst are asked to do something completely against the grain, which is to invite their demons to join them in the conversation. Most of what we call psychopathology is a consequence of the ways we try to keep the demons quiet. Analysts don't do therapy in order to confront their own demons, but the nature of the work requires them to do so.

One of the ways therapists try to keep the demons quiet is by fetishizing their theories. By focusing on more and more recondite formulations and terms, they shift their attention away from the unknown terrors that the clinical situation stirs up. This leads to the emergence of rival analytic churches debating the least important aspects of the psychoanalytic endeavor.

Trainees are particularly vulnerable to the appeal of the erudition of their mentors. Theoretical allegiances are often established well before trainees have a grasp of fundamental principles. Some cling to the conviction that,

DOI: 10.4324/9781003360391-1

once they master the theory, they will no longer experience anxiety in the inherently tense clinical encounter (Friedman, 1988, Chapter 1). Meanwhile, the trend seems to be to make the theories more and more obscure. I would favor a relatively simple model of the mind – e.g., without Greek letters – and a respect for the endless complexity of human experience. The difficulty should be in the practice, not in the language.

This leads me to my second impression. When therapists present their clinical work – for instance, in a continuous case conference – if the engagement seems genuine, it is usually not obvious that the work belongs to a particular school. The therapist will show a unique style in the treatment; it just isn't recognizable as, say, Kleinian or Freudian or Winnicottian. These seem to be names of group affiliations, of languages to explain the work rather than to describe the experience of the encounter. A large audience to a clinical presentation will often sort itself into groups that share points of approval or criticism of the presenter's work – but the groups will not correlate with the theoretical divisions; instead, they will align according to whether the therapist was empathic enough, or tough enough, too active or too quiet, and so on.

The analytic literature often conveys the subtext that analysts are inscrutably wise, remarkably clever, and unflappably patient. In written reports, emotional storms are aborted in an instant and replaced with life-altering insight in response to the analyst's crisp and pithy interpretation. This is likely not the writer's intent; no therapist would claim it to be a realistic picture of the analyst at work.

But the literature does not typically capture the actual experience of the analyst in the clinical situation. It tends to leave out the stumbling, lurching, always uncertain, sometimes terrifying intimacy of passionate engagement. It may convey a false impression of sterility, of detached study. The uncertainty, the therapist's anxiety, the tough slogging that leads incrementally to a shift of perception usually gets edited out.

My third impression has to do with the historical effort to define what is and what is not analysis. In Freud's lifetime it was important to him to distinguish analysis from other treatments – especially those espoused by his apostate disciples.

Unfortunately, the last time there was a consensus about what constitutes analysis, and what differentiates it from other therapies, was probably around 1900, when Freud was the only analyst. Nowadays, the practical answer to the question "What is analysis?" is the same as Justice Potter Stewart's definition of obscenity: I don't know how to define it, but I know it when I see it. Or, more frequently, I know what *I* do is analysis and what *you* do is not.

In 1920 the first psychoanalytic training institute was formed in Berlin. Since then, analytic institutes have served to teach analysis, and (until very recently) *only* analysis. This has the value of (apparent) clarity for trainees, among other advantages. But it has significant costs as well. One of the most profound is that it sets up "standards" by which students may be judged.[1] The notion itself seems laudable, but its execution is problematic. The idea of standards implies reproducibility of technical practice; that is, it suggests that trainees are learning a skill that can be applied by any analyst to all appropriate patients.

But psychic pain isn't gall bladder pain, and analysis isn't a cholecystectomy. What matters in analytic work is the encounter between two unique people, and most of what can be generalized in advance about such events is trivial.

This creates a problem for analytic outcome research, which seeks to compare the efficacy of analytic therapy to, say, cognitive behavioral therapy or escitalopram. In order to do so, simplifying assumptions are made – the most profoundly wrong-headed one being that analytic therapy is a reproducible event, independent of the particular participants.

More important to the practicing analyst, it creates a problem for training institutes: If we are teaching analysis, as distinct from anything else, students are under pressure to "do" analysis – and since the analytic encounter is irreproducible, they only have recourse to the trivial commonalities among analytic treatments, e.g., the use of the couch, the frequency, and whatever habits of analytic behavior they can pick up from case reports, to show that what they are doing is analysis. Thus they are encouraged to look and sound and act like analysts, even before they have a firm grasp of what they are trying to accomplish.

In the following pages I'll tell you my ideas. But who am I? From what I have already said, telling you I am an analyst says nothing about me. You would know more if I told you I am an excellent parallel parker and my biggest regret is never having done standup comedy. Psychoanalysis has been around for over a century, and analytic scholars can't even agree on what it is. We have definitions, of course; they usually (but not always) involve the relief of suffering through expanded self-awareness, achieved by talking with a person who understands something of how the mind works based on some of the discoveries of Sigmund Freud.

So who am I, and why should you care? What do I mean when I say I am an analyst? When prospective patients ask me what analysis is, I try to answer the question, and the question behind the question. I try to show them, based on what they are showing me, that they are doing something that contributes to their suffering. I tell them that there is a very good reason they continue to do so that we don't yet understand. I tell them that what they do is based on assumptions they make about how other people think and feel. I tell them that, if I can make this a safe place for them, together we can discover what their problematic actions buy them in terms of peace of mind and the assumptions on which that world-view is based. I tell them that, as we explore that territory together, they may be able to shift to a new and freer perspective. I tell them that it takes two of us, one inside their head and one out, and that my contribution is based on the skill to learn a lot about what it is like to be them without being them. Or words to that effect.

I also tell them that I haven't really told them what analysis is because I don't "do analysis" *to* them; I'm listening and thinking and feeling *with* them, based on who I am and what I understand about how minds work. I tell them we are going to learn from what we see ourselves doing with each other while we are talking. In short, when patients ask me what analysis is, I try to convey the message that this is how I think about what I do, but in any case I'll show you.

So here is what I'm telling you: I have a psychoanalytic model of the mind in mind that is fashioned after the ideas of Hans Loewald and aspects of the work of many others, incorporated both knowingly and unconsciously. But by now it should be clear that I am telling you how I prefer to see myself and what language I speak, not how I work. The model is a map, and the map is not the territory. In fact, with respect to analysis, the map may not even be the map – that is to say, how we work is not solely, nor even mainly, guided by our theorizing (see Chapter 12). No experienced analyst is a Freudian, or a Loewaldian, or a Kohutian, or an intersubjectivist. Each analyst, each patient, each analysis is *sui generis*.

As I reach the later stages of my career, the question of whether what I am doing is analysis has become less and less meaningful. I work analytically, by which I mean I have an idea of how people navigate their lives that shapes how I listen. The idea comes from theory to some degree, but to a much greater extent it comes from who I am and where I've been. I try to follow rather than to lead. I try to feel with the patient and to think about the encounter. What I actually do depends on my patient. Finally, my answer to who am I is the same as I tell my patients: I'll show you.

I can now rephrase those three impressions from the beginning. Emphasis on increasingly complex theorizing is often misused to protect the therapist against the threatening intensity of the clinical encounter, to the detriment of the latter. An analyst's theory has much less to do with her actual clinical work than we think. And the analytic literature is inadvertently encouraging a false ideal of clinical detachment, while rarely conveying the passions and terrors of genuine clinical engagement.

In what follows I will respond to these impressions, though in a necessarily incomplete fashion. I will begin in Part I by considering the people that come to us for help. It is my view that diagnostic hair-splitting is a version of the defensive theorizing I mentioned above, and as such it is counterproductive. Accordingly, I have reduced diagnostic considerations to three categories into which all of us fall: neurotic, perverse, and psychotic. I introduce the concept of the syntax of thought to describe the variations of thinking and experiencing characteristic of each category. Along the way I offer a clarification of the term *sadomasochism* (Chapter 6) that I think adds to its clinical value.

In Part II I take up the matter of how to think about what the analyst is doing while analyzing. I try to show the clinical utility of attending to the interaction and to the syntax of the patient's thought. I argue that, no matter the theoretical approach, there is more nonanalytic influence going on in the action between the participants than the theory describes or the analyst notices. I look at the disparity between our espoused theories and our actual practice. I conclude by challenging the very idea of a technique for psychoanalysis.

In Part III I consider some of what goes on in the heart and mind of the analyst, usually described as empathy and countertransference. Part IV takes up two complementary abilities: the capacity to immerse oneself in action and the capacity to step back and reflect on the action. I argue that these paired capacities are at the center of the analyst's ability to work as an analyst and the patient's ability to work optimally as a patient.

In the Coda, I take on the psychoanalytic literature directly, first by reasoned discourse, then by satire.

This book covers issues I have grappled with in my office over the past 40 years. I hope it will give therapists a fresh angle on their own work.

Why should you care? Well, you've come this far. If you still don't care, I won't take it personally.

Note

1 For a comprehensive study of the dangers of institutionalizing analysis, see Reeder (2004). For a more impassioned study, see Roustang (1982).

References

Friedman, L. (1988). *The anatomy of psychotherapy*. Analytic Press.

Reeder, J. (2004). *Hate and love in psychoanalytical institutions: The dilemma of a profession*. Other Press.

Roustang, F. (1982). *Dire mastery. Discipleship from Freud to Lacan*. Johns Hopkins.

Part I

With Whom Do We Do What We Do?

When I was a psychiatric resident, fresh from reading Otto Kernberg, I sought consultation with a supervisor on a "borderline" patient. She immediately stopped me, objecting to the diagnostic term. She said, "I only have two bins: neurotic and psychotic." I immediately had a mental picture of the bins – more like dumpsters – into which my supervisor was bodily sorting her caseload.

There is something dehumanizing about diagnosis, as with any other kind of stereotyping. Diagnosis, after all, involves putting disparate individuals into a "bin" by finding shared characteristics and ignoring differences. A diagnosis is a class, not a person. In medicine, in my lifetime at least, doctors have tended to proceed as if they are treating diagnoses rather than people. As the philosopher Maurice Natanson (personal communication) put it, "Doctors would prefer you to send in the diseased part, and leave the rest of you at home."

For psychoanalysts, the subject of clinical attention is the person interacting with the analyst. The diagnosis is less for the consulting room and more for reflecting on clinical experience, for teaching, consulting, and supervising. It is a way to talk about clinical problems with other clinicians.

It is with that proviso that I begin by describing my bins: neurotic, psychotic, and other. I think these three categories convey three radically different worlds in which people live. I have found that familiarity with their essentials is useful for preparing oneself to work with the endless variations on being human that we encounter in practice.

It is worth mentioning that diagnostic categories are not moral assessments – although they may include implications about the individual's own contradictory moral positions. As Poland (2018) put it, Freud's mistake was not calling his 1901 book *The Psychodynamics of Everyday Life*. The bins are not good, fair, and poor; and I don't have a bin for "normal," because there isn't any normal, any ideal of mental health. There are only varieties of human experience. Ultimately, we treat suffering, not psychopathology.

I begin this section with three chapters about neurotic processes. Neurotically organized people struggle in a fashion for which analysis was

DOI: 10.4324/9781003360391-2

invented as a treatment. I define neurosis as suffering as a consequence of successful repression. I emphasize the syntax of neurotic thinking.

In Chapters 4 and 5 I take up the "other" category. Freud had made all his major clinical contributions by 1926. After that, he struggled with only one other clinical problem. On returning to his earlier work on men with sexual perversions, he reconsidered people who (as I imagine it) seemed to accept his interpretations and then not do anything with them in their lives. He saw that these men were fully capable of distinguishing the real from the imaginary and therefore were not psychotic; yet they seemed to be particularly tolerant of the contradictions between their fantasies and reality.

Given the context in which Freud elaborated this capacity to disavow troubling reality and to distinguish it from neurosis or psychosis, I have followed the lead of Arlow (1971) and called this "other" category *perverse* (Chapter 4), and the term has caught on. I am not altogether happy with that choice, since perverse processes are far more common than frank sexual perversion, and their prevalence is not demographically skewed toward one gender (as far as I can tell). But I have not come up with a good alternative. Arthur Bloch (2002) has written a spoof of a self-help book called *Healing Yourself with Wishful Thinking*. Maybe *wishful thinkers* would be a better name for people in this category.

Diagnostic splitters use terms such as borderline, narcissistic, panphobic, pseudoneurotic, sociopathic, and "serious character pathology" to describe some of the members of this group. They tend to irritate analysts, as they make it difficult to practice "pure" analysis. They also tend to evoke the most intense reactions of either sadomasochism or withdrawal.

I define this group as people who suffer as a consequence of the inability to use repression successfully. As with neurosis, I try to articulate the syntax of perverse thought as I understand it.

Chapter 6 takes up a reformulation of sadomasochism. I distinguish it from aggression by its effort to preserve a tie to an object. Sadomasochistic relating is a transitional point in the development of object relations, in that the object is understood to be "not me," but it is not a fully independent person to the subject. Its manifestations are seen in perverse and (regressively) in neurotic organizations as the need to control an object.

Chapter 7 is a note on work with a psychotic woman, to which I was more witness than participant. Despite the patient's presence on the couch, I would be astonished if anyone were to describe it as analysis. But it does provide an example from which to consider the syntax of psychotic thought.

Many will note the absence of a category for depression. I think of depression, and narcissism as well, as occurring in people of all three categories. In other words, neurotic depression is syntactically organized (or "structured") along neurotic lines, and perverse and psychotic depression follow the syntax of perversion and psychosis, respectively.

I end this section with a brief note on the nature of the dramas enacted in treatment with members of each category.

References

Arlow, J.A. (1971). Character perversion. In I.W. Marcus (Ed.), *Currents in psycho-analysis* (pp. 317–36). International Universities Press.

Bloch, A. (2002). *Healing yourself with wishful thinking.* Ten Speed Press.

Poland, W.S. (2018). *Intimacy and separateness in psychoanalysis.* Routledge.

Chapter 1

Neurosis as a Way of Thinking

The Syntax of Unconscious Oedipal Thought

In this chapter I introduce the concept of "syntax of thought," to which I will return in subsequent chapters. My usage of the word *syntax* is admittedly idiosyncratic. Its proper use refers to sentence structure, and indeed there are times when thought is expressed in sentences, spoken or implied, as in Chapter 9. But what I am trying to convey as the syntax of thought also has implications about the nature of the world in which the subject lives. In the psychotic extreme (see Chapter 7), thoughts expressed in words are physical things with physical impact.

In the more than fifty years since Bion's (1970) "thoughts without a thinker," psychoanalysis has enjoyed a rapid expansion of thinking about thinking. In an effort to push the boundaries of our grasp of human experience to earlier and earlier points in development, many contributors have enriched our understanding of prelogical and preverbal thought, including such concepts as unmentalized experience (Mitrani, e.g., 1995), protoemotions (Ferro, 2012), a core self (Stern, e.g., 1985), and mentalization (Fonagy, e.g., 1991). Primitive mental states have been explored to great therapeutic advantage by Alvarez (e.g., 2006), Williams (e.g., 2004), Ogden (e.g., 1989), Roussillon (e.g., 2010), and many others too numerous to mention.

During these same years, there appears to have been waning interest in the concept of neurosis, and with it an unfortunate neglect of the distinctive form of thinking that characterizes neurotic functioning. By 1980, the American Psychiatric Association's diagnostic manual eliminated the term altogether. Hinshelwood (1991) has no entry for neurosis in his *A Dictionary of Kleinian Thought*; the one time the word "neurotic" is used, it is in quotes, as if to indicate the quaintness of the term (p. 417). The *Psychodynamic Diagnostic Manual* (PDM Task Force, 2006) uses it only adjectivally, as a quantitative measure of seriousness, as "neurotic-level personality disorder" (pp. 23–4).

In what follows I will revisit the concept of neurosis in order to place it in the context of the present-day interest in the classes of adult mentation. I will identify neurotic thinking with repressed oedipal-phase-appropriate thinking and try to sort out some of its consequential attributes. My hope is to reinsert

DOI: 10.4324/9781003360391-3

neurosis into our contemporary theorizing about the development of thinking and its contribution to the form of adult suffering.

Freud's Usage

Freud adopted the term neurosis some thirty years before his model of the mind evolved into its final form. His developmental theory began as an unfolding sequence of modes of libidinal satisfaction, and, although he may have implied a role for what we might now call ego functions, it was not until the introduction of the structural model (1923) and the revision of anxiety theory (1926) that he had laid the groundwork to consider the development of thinking itself. Freud listed as one of his goals in the Little Hans case (1909), to "consider whether it can be made to shed any light upon the mental life of children" (p. 101), but he never returned to that project in earnest. I will pursue that goal in the next chapter.

The fact that Freud thought of Hans's phobia as a neurotic symptom and never revised that view has, I think, contributed to the imprecise use of the term. At the time, Freud used the term "repression" in the Hans case in the generic sense of "defense" – but he was not referring to the active process of forgetting and keeping forgotten that would be its later redefinition (1926, p. 163). Indeed, it would be hard to demonstrate an instance of repression proper in the Hans case. Freud did distinguish between the adult neurosis and the underlying "infantile neurosis," but one of the implications of my position is that the "infantile neurosis" is not, strictly speaking, a neurosis, precisely because its "contents" are not repressed.

It is worth noting that, in his paper "Primitive emotional development," Winnicott (1945, pp. 145–56), a pioneer in conceptualizing the mental life of the youngest infants and the most severely disturbed adults, described "different types of psychoanalysis" (p. 146). He wrote,

> It is possible to do the analysis *of a suitable patient* taking into account almost exclusively that person's personal relation to people, along with the conscious and unconscious fantasies that enrich and complicate these relationships between whole persons. This is the original type of psycho-analysis .... It is right for a student analyst to learn first to cope with ambivalence in external relationships and with simple repression and then to progress to the analysis of [depressive and primitive pre-depressive relationships].
>
> (Winnicott, 1945, pp. 146–7; italics added)

Winnicott's syndrome of "ambivalence" (as a capacity), "simple repression," and a capacity for relationships with "whole persons" is a fair definition of neurosis. Thus, a neurotic was a suitable patient for the "original type" of analysis. On this point he was in agreement with Freud (1924, p. 203), who saw analysis as a treatment for neurosis.[1]

Neurotic Thought

In one sentence, neurosis is a form of suffering resulting from the effects of repression. Why and how that should be a class has to do with the state of development of thinking that holds sway at the time of the far-reaching repression that occasions the end of the oedipal phase and ushers in latency (Freud, 1923). In the adult, the sign of that massive repression is retrograde infantile amnesia.

Let us turn now to how the child thinks during the oedipal phase. The premise I am putting forward is that *what is locked in by the repression that marks the end of the oedipal phase is a view of human relationship that is cast in the syntax of oedipal thought*. Here are some of the relevant features of the syntax of oedipal thought:[2]

First, in the course of normal-enough development, the oedipal-phase child will have developed a capacity to anticipate future scenarios based on her age-specific theory of cause and effect. The causal theory will be "egocentric," in Piaget's (Sandler, 1975, p. 369) use of the term; that is, important events will be construed by the child as having been caused by her activities. A corollary to this point is that the oedipal child does not believe there is such a thing as an accident.

Second, the child at this stage will have considerable access to sexual and aggressive urges; or, to put it differently, she will not yet have successfully repressed them. Conversely, by the end of this phase the child will have developed a sufficient capacity for repression – that is, for actively forgetting "dangerous" thoughts – such that they can be (relatively) successfully excluded from preconscious availability.

Third, the child at this stage will not have firmly consolidated the ability to differentiate between thought and action (that is, between "psychic" and "external" reality). This blurred distinction is the basis for the so-called "omnipotence of thought."[3]

Fourth, the child at this stage will recognize others as independent agents; that is, she will have developed the capacity for full object relations. But despite that achievement, the child at this stage will assume that the motives of others are identical to her own.

When development reaches the point where the above conditions occur together, and the child (inevitably) finds a reason to imagine dire consequences should her sexual and/or aggressive wishes come to pass, she will have powerful motivation to put her omnipotent thoughts out of mind. This is the repression that results in the infantile amnesia (Freud, 1909, p.149) and entry into the latency period. At about the same time, internalization of aspects of relations with the parents creates the superego. In contrast to repression, which fixes oedipal syntax in a way that escapes further maturation, internalizations are fluid and less stable. The balance between repression and internalization is fateful for future development. A tilt toward repression will predispose toward neurotic inhibition, and a tilt toward internalization will predispose toward instability.

It is the role of repressed *oedipal-phase-specific thinking* – the confluence of egocentricity, confusion of thought and action manifested as belief in the omnipotence of thought, and attribution of one's own motives to others – that provides the conditions for an adult neurosis: terror at the possibility of experiencing certain thoughts and feelings about a loved one, motivating the maintenance of the repression and mobilizing defenses to deal with the threat of the "return of the repressed" (Freud, 1915, p. 154).[4] The syntax of neurotic thought is the syntax of repressed oedipal thought.

A Clinical Sketch

I will not provide a detailed clinical illustration for two reasons. First, the kinds of deductions I am making are routine and familiar to most analysts. Second, however plausible these inferences might be, they are just that: inferences about unconscious thought. That means either I would need to provide immense detail and context in order to be convincing or I would have to resort to the "analysis showed" formula. But for the purposes of clarifying without trying to provide evidence of anything, I will illustrate what I have been saying in a clinical context.

A recently married cardiologist, Dr. C, came for a consultation about two new problems: She had lost interest in sex with her husband, and she had developed a fear of driving across bridges. She told me immediately about the bridge between her home city and the hospital where she works. She loves her work, but she is so terrified as she approaches the bridge that she has to turn around and go home. She had driven across the bridge daily for some years before, without a second thought. She reported that her interest in sex with her husband had been robust, if a little tame for her tastes, until recently.

The two problems began more or less simultaneously. When I asked about the "tame" sex, she noted that she had found sex with her husband (and with others) more exciting before she married him. A discussion of her excitement led her to add that she had recently begun to flirt with a co-worker in a way that both thrilled and troubled her. She felt swept up in something. Although the timing fit the onset of symptoms perfectly, she had not made the connection between the flirtation and the phobia.

The only daughter of a rather arrogant physician father and a timid and inhibited mother, Dr. C was witness to frequent fights that apparently involved the father demeaning the mother. Dr. C soon remembered how enthralled she was with her father and the disdain she had for her mother, although this first showed itself when Dr. C talked of worrying about her mother. In first grade she developed a school phobia, frequently requiring the mother's presence in the classroom. At age eight her parents divorced; after an ugly custody fight she was sent to live with her father.

Here are the kinds of inferences that one might make about oedipal thinking from the above sketch: As an oedipal child, Dr. C was convinced that her father loved her more than he did her mother (unrepressed desire, omnipotence of thought, whole objects as suggested by the triadic relations). She was convinced that she was hurting her mother (unrepressed aggression, omnipotence of thought). She was convinced that she would end up with her father (anticipating the future), while at the same time she imagined being left by her mother as a punishment (attribution of motives, whole object relations). It did not occur to her that their problems were theirs and not about her (Piagetian "egocentrism"). The divorce "confirmed" her oedipal convictions that her wishes had injured her mother by taking her father away. The fear of the power of her thoughts motivated the repression that ushered in latency.

The new flirtation in adulthood had stirred up a "return of the repressed," with her taking her father's role (as she had done more or less effectively in her character, her career choice, and her marriage up until then). This led to the new sexual excitement and also an upsurge of anxiety around hurting her husband that gained strength from her oedipal convictions (the excitement itself was dangerous, a derivative of the omnipotence of thought). Her phobic symptom regulated her anxiety by displacing it to a safer object and inhibiting her access to the co-worker.

Let me repeat that this example is not intended to prove anything; rather, it is meant to show what I mean by oedipal thinking and how it manifests itself in neurosis. It does not matter if my inferences are correct, but I hope the nature of the inferential process will be recognizable to analysts who work with neurotic people.

Repression and Oedipal Thought

Neurotic symptomatology and character structure (as well as most of asymptomatic functioning) in the adult depend on relatively successful repression to keep conscious mental life relatively free of sexual and aggressive preoccupations, at the cost of locking in the oedipal-phase beliefs that lead to symptom formation. At the heart of any adult neurosis is the conviction that some thoughts cause disastrous effects. Finally, that is the motive for the repression that brings an end to the conscious oedipal struggles, creates the infantile amnesia, and inaugurates the latency period.

Once that fateful event occurs, accompanied and facilitated by the parental identifications involved in forming the superego, consciousness is available for other tasks. But once that event occurs, the repressed "complex," *organized in the way of thinking at the time of the repression*, is no longer accessible to further maturation. In other words, it is not just the oedipal desires that are repressed; it is also the belief in the omnipotence of thought and the egocentric theory of causality that were age-appropriate, for example in Little Hans (see next chapter). These islands of magical thinking about the consequences of certain forbidden thoughts, now dynamically unconscious, remain unaffected by the otherwise ongoing developmental flow. They form the nucleus of neurotic symptoms and character traits in the adult.

Non-Neurotic Psychic Organization

We do meet many nonpsychotic adults who do not use repression very successfully and who handle their resultant (preconsciously available) urges predominantly with disavowal, negation, distraction or fixation of attention, perceptual alteration, wishful thinking, and dishonesty. But we do not call such people neurotic; their ego and superego functioning has more in common with perversion and sociopathy than with neurosis.

I will take up what I think of as perverse organization in more depth in Chapters 4 and 5. But to distinguish it from neurosis, we may recall Freud's (1905) dictum that perversion is the negative of neurosis. His statement was based on his idea of intrapsychic conflict and the structure of the resultant compromise formation: In neurosis, a wish is altered or inhibited in order to allow partial gratification while satisfying the demands of (the superego's assessment of) reality, whereas in perversion (and related phenomena) the assessment of realistic dangers is altered in order to allow gratification of the relatively unmodified wish.

Furthermore, in perverse processes, anxiety is handled typically by keeping preconsciously available (that is, unrepressed) elements separate. It is to describe the isolation of unintegrated yet unrepressed ideas that the term "splitting" has evolved, beginning with Freud's "splitting of the ego" (e.g., 1927) and including the Kleinian and Kohutian ("vertical split," 1971) versions.

Summary and Concluding Remarks

I have tried to show how neurosis can be understood as the type of difficulty that arises from the effect of the massive repression that ushers in latency. Not only is it the case that repression locks in infantile sources of gratification to which a vulnerable person may regress; more importantly, it also locks in the mode of relating and the syntax of thought that are active at the time of the repression. For more or less successful repression to occur, development has to have proceeded adequately to the point that the child has entered into the oedipal phase. Just as the features of primitive mentation dictate the structure of so-called primitive symptomatology, the characteristic syntax of oedipal thinking determines the structure of adult neurosis.

Notes

1 Winnicott was not implying that neurotic patients were free of more primitive pathology "which one can surely find in any analysis" (1945, p. 147). That notion, along with the related idea of a "psychotic core," deserves a book of its own.
2 This list owes a great deal to the ideas of Anne-Marie Sandler (1975) and her application of Piaget's work.
3 Freud used the phrase *omnipotence of thought* to refer specifically to sadistic or destructive obsessional fantasies, but it follows that it is always some version of a belief in the magical power of thinking that motivates repression and other defenses to prevent it.
4 The logic and syntax of oedipal thinking corresponds reasonably well with Piaget's (1959; Inhelder & Piaget, 1958) "preoperational" thinking – the clinically relevant aspects of which are summarized earlier in the paragraph.

References

Alvarez, A. (2006). Some questions concerning states of fragmentation: Unintegration, under-integration, disintegration, and the nature of early integrations. *Journal of Child Psychotherapy*, 32(2), 158–80.

American Psychiatric Association (1980). *Diagnostic and statistical manual of mental disorders* (3rd ed.). American Psychiatric Association.

Bion, W.R. (1970). *Attention and interpretation: A scientific approach to insight in psychoanalysis and groups*. Tavistock.

Ferro, A. (2012). Creativity in the consulting room: Factors of fertility and infertility. *Psychoanalytic Inquiry*, 32(3), 257–74.

Fonagy, P. (1991). Thinking about thinking: Some clinical and theoretical considerations in the treatment of a borderline patient. *The International Journal of Psychoanalysis*, 72(4), 639–56.

Freud, S. (1905). Three essays on the theory of sexuality. SE 7, 125–321.

Freud, S. (1909). Analysis of a phobia in a five-year-old boy. SE 7, 3–152.

Freud, S. (1915). Repression. SE *14*, 141–58.

Freud, S. (1923). *The Ego and the Id*. SE *19*, 3–68.

Freud, S. (1924). A short account of psycho-analysis. SE *19*, 189–210.

Freud, S. (1926). *Inhibitions, Symptoms, and Anxiety*. SE *20*, 77–178.

Freud, S. (1927). Fetishism. SE *21*, 147–58.

Hinshelwood, R.D. (1991). *A dictionary of Kleinian thought* (2nd ed). Jason Aronson.

Inhelder, B., & Piaget, J. (1958). *The growth of logical thinking from childhood to adolescence* (A. Parsons & S. Milgram, Trans.). Basic Books.

Kohut, H. (1971). *The analysis of the self*. International Universities Press.

Mitrani, J.L. (1995). Toward an understanding of unmentalized experience. *The Psychoanalytic Quarterly*, 64(1), 68–112.

Ogden, T.H. (1989). *The primitive edge of experience*. Jason Aronson.

PDM Task Force (2006). *Psychodynamic diagnostic manual (PDM)*. Alliance of Psychoanalytic Organizations.

Piaget, J. (1959). *The language and thought of the child* (M. Gabain & R. Gabain, Trans.; 2nd ed.). Routledge and Kegan Paul.

Roussillon, R. (2010). The deconstruction of primary narcissism. *The International Journal of Psychoanalysis*, *91*(4), 821–37.

Sandler, A.-M. (1975). Comments on the significance of Piaget's work for psychoanalysis. *International Review of Psycho-Analysis*, *2*(4), 365–77.

Stern, D.N. (1985). *The interpersonal world of the infant*. Basic Books.

Williams, P. (2004). Symbols and self preservation in severe disturbance. *Journal of Analytical Psychology*, *49*(1), 21–31.

Winnicott, D.W. (1945). *Through paediatrics to psycho-analysis*. Hogarth Press and Institute of Psycho-Analysis (1978).

Chapter 2

The Syntax of Oedipal Thought in the Case of Little Hans

Now that I have introduced the idea of oedipal syntax, I would like to return to Freud's one and only extended look at an oedipal child. Herbert Graf, the son of Freud's friend Max Graf, is known in the case history as Little Hans.

"The Analysis of a Phobia in a Five-(Year-Old Boy" (Freud, 1909) is now into its second century of study. It has rightly been called a "founding text" (Young-Bruehl, 2007), the "prototype of child analysis," (Blum, 2007, p. 59), and the first record of child analytic supervision (Bierman, 2007, p. 92) – the treatment was conducted by Hans's father, in consultation with Freud. Freud's main goal in reporting the case was to test his ideas on infantile sexuality (Freud, 1909, p. 101). Although he listed as a secondary goal to "consider whether [the case] can be made to shed any light upon the mental life of children" (p. 101), he did not seem to note the role of Hans's phase-specific thinking in shaping his phobia. In this chapter I will try to show how careful attention to Hans's language and syntax illustrates the nature of oedipal-phase thought and its contribution to pathogenesis.

Freud's report is unique for its time in many ways, even beyond the age of the patient and the fact that the father is the treating analyst. The abundance of verbatim exchanges in particular provides opportunities to draw inferences beyond those of the analyst or consultant. Also, the report follows the "development and resolution of a phobia in a boy *under* five years of age"[1] (Freud, 1909, p. 101; italics added), *progressively*, beginning with premorbid observations and continuing as a real-time record of the onset of the phobic symptom and the treatment. It is not a reconstruction. The state of Freud's theory *circa* 1909 emphasized the epigenetic sequencing of psychosexual stages organized around erotogenic zones. In this historical context Freud was satisfied that he had succeeded in demonstrating the libidinal and aggressive elements that defined the Oedipus complex. He saw Hans's complex as the model of the source from which adult neuroses were derived

Although Freud noted aspects of how Hans's mind worked, his interest at the time was with Hans's conclusions – that is, the content of his fantasies – as a contribution to libido theory. Beyond the role of the age-appropriate

DOI: 10.4324/9781003360391-4

psychosexual stage and (to some degree) the interaction of his libidinal urges with the environment, he did not take up the question of Hans's developmentally appropriate capacities and vulnerabilities and how they shaped the world as he experienced it. I think most analysts have filled in the blanks since then, but I would like to pursue the information that is available in Freud's own report in order to show how oedipal-phase *thinking* contributed to Hans's difficulties at least as much as his oedipal *conflicts*.

As outlined in the previous chapter, the characteristics of oedipal-age thought on which I would like to focus are as follows:

1.   In the course of normal development, the child of Hans's age will have achieved a reasoning ability that allows her to envision future scenarios based on her age-specific theory of cause and effect.
2.   The theory in question will be "egocentric," in Piaget's (Sandler, 1975, p. 369) use of the term; that is, important events will be construed by the child as having been caused by her activities.
3.   The child at this stage will have considerable conscious access to sexual and aggressive urges; or, to put it differently, she will not yet have successfully repressed them.
4.   The child at this stage will not have firmly consolidated the ability to differentiate between thought and action (that is, between "psychic" and "external" reality).
5.   The child at this stage will assume that the motives of others are identical to her own.

My undertaking this task does not seem to me to be a novel contribution. It is consistent, for example, with A.-M. Sandler's (1975) position, and I think the findings are familiar to contemporary child analysts and observers. I am merely suggesting that these factors can be found even in this very early work, even when its author was not looking for them.

One may ask why these questions have not been taken up in discussions of Little Hans already. I believe three factors may have contributed to the difficulty. First, as noted, in 1909 Freud's interest was in the state of infantile sexuality manifested in the Oedipus complex and not in the ego's capacities and limitations therein. Second, Freud's theory at the time was still the notion that anxiety was the effect of, rather than the motive for, "repression." Because of that theory, when he noted anxiety, he presumed repression.[2] Third, as I mentioned in the last chapter, at that time Freud used the word "repression" in the generic sense that we now use the word "defense"; he would not give it a more specific meaning until 1926 (Freud, 1926, p. 105), when he would also officially revise his anxiety theory (Freud, 1926, p. 93). This leads to a good deal of confusion for readers, as it seems that much of what Freud calls "repression" in the case has to do with the conscious deployment of attention for defensive purposes, rather than the motivated forgetting that is exemplified so dramatically by the infantile amnesia that Freud had noted as early as 1901 (Freud, 1901, p. 46).

In addition to these three factors, there is also some ambiguity in how Freud uses the term "unconscious" in his report. At times he seems to be using Hans's lack of attention to an idea as evidence that it is unconscious — i.e., he conflates the descriptive unconscious with the dynamic unconscious (1923, p. 15).

With these complexities in mind, I will now turn to a few selections from Freud's report in an effort to demonstrate some of the points about oedipal-phase thinking that I listed above. Among the tools we have at our disposal, I would like to draw special attention to clues offered by the syntax of Hans's own statements.

The Syntax of Dream, Fantasy, and Fable

Consider Hans's language when he describes a dream: "Last night I thought" (Freud, 1909, p. 19). "When I was asleep, I thought" (p. 23). It is not clear what "thought" is to him, or what truth value he assigns to it. At the very least we may infer that the distinction between dreaming and lived experience is not yet firmly consolidated. Hans does have some distinction in mind between dreaming and thinking. On one occasion he entered his parents' bedroom. The next morning when his father asked why, Hans told an elaborate story that began, "In the night there was a big giraffe in the room" (p. 37). When his father asked if he had dreamed it, Hans said "No, I didn't dream it. I thought it. I thought it all. I'd woken up earlier" (p. 37). It is in fact unclear whether this was a dream or a waking fantasy, and, from Freud's perspective at the time, the distinction was not very important. But we may surmise that the distinction had a different meaning to Hans than the adult version, and/or that its meaning may have been very fluid. At any rate, we should note that Hans's syntax suggests that he experienced the thoughts as an event, rather than as an imaginary creation.

Perhaps more revealing is the syntax of Hans's waking thoughts and daydreams. For example, when he describes his fear that a horse would bite him, Hans adds, "The horse'll come into the room" (p. 24), as if he considered it a real possibility. Hans described what Freud identified as a masturbation fantasy "equivalent to a dream" (p. 32) as follows: "I *saw* Mummy .... I *showed* Grete ... I *saw* [Mummy's] widdler" (p. 32; italics added). Note the action verbs; Hans is treating the "fantasy" as actual events.

At several points Hans tells fantastic stories, often long and involved ones, in which he rapidly switches his ground about what he claims to be true. In one such fable, he adds, "Really and truly I can remember quite well ... My word of honour! ... I'm not joking" (Freud, 1909, pp. 69–70). Freud attributes the lying to Hans avenging himself for the father's fabrications about the stork bringing babies (pp. 69–70). But with respect to other confabulations, Hans interposes, "I say, what I'm telling you isn't a bit true" (p. 77; see also pp. 80, 85). On one occasion Hans's father reports the following exchange:

I: "Have you ever teased horses?"
HANS: "Yes, quite often. I'm afraid I shall do it, but I don't really .... Once I really did it. Once I had the whip and whipped the horse .... What I've told you isn't the least true .... I've thought it to myself" (Freud, 1909, pp. 79–80).

It seems here that Hans is grappling with the distinction between wishing and acting (and, relatedly, between truth and falsehood) with limited success. He "knows" the difference; e.g., after his father observes (accuses him?) that Hans still wants to touch his widdler, Hans replies "But wanting's not doing and doing's not wanting" (Freud, 1909, p. 31). But his faith in this distinction only seems to come up in a defensive way and tends to evaporate. In this instance, it seems likely that he has in fact continued to masturbate, but he is trying to tell himself he wasn't "doing" anything by (correctly) parsing the distinction. In an even more lawyerlike example, after Hans freely acknowledges his preference that his sister not be alive, his father tells Hans, "A good boy doesn't wish that sort of thing." Hans answers, "But he may THINK it" (p. 72, emphasis in the original). Here Hans seems to be distinguishing intention (wishing for) and "neutral" hypothesizing. He makes an even more challenging distinction later on, when considering the wish that his mother should have a baby:

HANS: "But I don't want it to happen."
I: "But you wish for it?"
HANS: "Oh yes, *wish*." (Freud, 1909, p. 92; italics in original).

It may be that Hans is distinguishing wishing and wanting on the basis of intensity; or it may be that he is expressing conflicting wishes. I will not pursue the first possibility, but I will return to the second idea later.

Causation and Egocentrism

Children Hans's age normally realize that actions have consequences, but (as we see in Hans) the definition of "action" is expandable to include thoughts and wishes, and the consequences don't always make adult sense. Oedipal children don't believe in accidents and seem unable to believe that they could be innocent bystanders. In Hans's case we learn that his phobia worsened following his tonsillectomy (Freud, 1909, p. 29). When his father tells him he is worse because his illness prevented him from going for walks, Hans corrects him: "Oh no. It's so bad because I still put my hand to my widdler every night" (p. 30). It seems plausible that Hans construed his "having his tonsils cut" (p. 29) as a punishment for his sexual urges as well.[3]

Central to the theory of cause and effect typical of Hans's age is the kind of self-centeredness that Piaget (Sandler, 1975, p. 369) called "egocentrism." The capacity to appreciate motives of others that differ from our own is a relatively late developmental accomplishment. A "developmental line" (A. Freud, 1963) for object relations would begin in some undifferentiated or narcissistic state and pass through a sadomasochistic phase on the way to full appreciation for the independent other. Hans recognizes and appreciates objects, but he infers their motives by assuming them to be identical with his own. Hans displays his age-appropriate egocentrism after admitting that he wished his father would fall down and be hurt. When his father asks why, Hans replies, "Because you're cross" (Freud, 1909, p. 82). When his father says it is not true, Hans responds, "Yes, it *is* true. You're cross. I know you are. It must be true" (p. 83; italics in original). Any adult might make the same misattribution (or projection), but the certainty about it, appropriate to a four-year-old, might be considered paranoid in the adult.

Repression and Defense

As noted above, the word "repression" appears throughout Freud's report, but he uses it in the generic sense for which he would later substitute the word "defense." In fact, it appears that repression proper is more conspicuous by its absence than its use in Hans. Consider, for example, his usual response to his father's deep interpretive confrontations and questions: "Yes, that's right" (Freud, 1909, p. 40), or simply "Yes" (pp. 67, 90). In answer to a direct question about his sister, Hans said "I'd rather she weren't alive" (p. 71). These statements are made so matter-of-factly that one can almost imagine Hans adding "So what's your point?" He is very frank and open, both about his intention to marry his mother (p. 92) and about his thought that "if only Daddy were to die [Hans would] be Daddy" (p. 90) – one of his father's interpretations to which he responded simply "yes" (p. 90). In fact, the clearest example of repression in the contemporary sense comes in the postscript, in which Freud notes that the *adolescent* Hans had no recollection of his phobia or of the treatment – it had all been overtaken by the infantile amnesia (p. 149).

Neubauer (2007) implies that Freud was aware of the conscious availability of Hans's conflicts, as illustrated by Freud's first suggested interpretation of the phobia: "The truth was, his father was to say, that [Hans] was very fond of his mother and wanted to be taken into her bed. The reason he was afraid of horses now was that he had taken so much interest in their widdlers" (Freud, 1909, p. 28). Neubauer comments, "Freud's recommended interpretation is startlingly direct; apparently, he felt he had no need to address the role of resistances or to elicit free associations. And indeed, Hans was so open at this point to face his conflict, *so conscious of it*, that the interpretation offered was not only accepted without signs of resistance but was rewarded by Hans offering additional memories" (Neubauer, 2007, p. 148; italics added).

Hans does demonstrate a repertory of defensive maneuvers, but for the most part they are directed against what is preconsciously available – in other words, they involve alterations in attention (negation, disavowal, displacement, turning away, not noticing) or alterations in perception (condensation, confusion of dream and waking states, confusion of fact and fiction). We have seen some examples of the perceptual alterations already. As for the deployment of attention, the first obvious example is the phobia itself, in which feelings toward the father are displaced onto horses. (I do not think the repression expected to accompany adult phobias has been demonstrated in Hans). The simplest instance was of looking away from the phobic object (Freud, 1909, p. 33). Among the other perceptual alterations, the plainest was Hans "seeing" his sister's widdler (e.g., pp. 11, 14, 21, 32, 62). We hear the negation in Hans's statement to himself, "Everyone has a widdler .... It's fixed in, of course" (p. 34).

Conscious Contradictory Ideas

Earlier I cited a moment in which Hans said he did not want something, but he wished for it (Freud, 1909, p. 92). Hans exhibits a remarkable tolerance for contradiction. Discussing Hans's ambivalence toward his father, Freud noted, "In the adult these pairs of contrary emotions do not as a rule become simultaneously conscious .... But in children they can exist peaceably side by side for quite a considerable time" (p. 113). At another point in the case report Hans says to his father, "I should so like to have children; but I don't ever want it; I shouldn't like to have them" (p. 93). Freud footnotes, "This startling contradiction was one between phantasy and reality, between wishing and having. Hans knew that in reality he was a child and that the other children would only be in his way; but in phantasy he was a mother and wanted children with whom he could repeat the endearments that he had himself experienced" (p. 93, footnote 2). This explanation would certainly fit the earlier wishing/wanting conflict as well, although the phrase "in reality" is not unambiguous in the world of the four-year-old – the progressive differentiation of fantasy and reality (Abrams, 1984, pp. 94–95) is one of the tasks of the oedipal phase. But for our purposes, the important feature of the contradictory ideas is that, as Freud noted about the ambivalence, they are *entirely conscious*.

In a neurotic adult, an internally prohibited wish might be repressed while its repudiation remained conscious. In a prelatency child, absent effective repression, the two sides of the conflict often coexist by virtue of the child's refraining from pursuing the significance of the wishes. I believe this to be the proper meaning of Freud's term "disavowal" (*verleugnung*). Hans thinks one thought, then the other; he does not trouble himself with reconciling the two. We would expect that, as development proceeds, the imperative to settle the issue would grow as the child's capacity to imagine a causal chain with dire consequences grows. This may coincide with Piaget's concrete operational stage. In any case, we do not get to follow Hans that far.

The Syntax of the Compromise

We are told by Freud that Hans found a successful solution to his Oedipus complex with the plumber fantasy (Freud, 1909, p. 98): He gets a bigger widdler and a bigger behind, and his father gets to marry his own mother (Hans's grandmother). In discussing this with his father, Hans adds, "I'd like to have a mustache like yours and hairs like yours" (p. 98). Let us underscore two features about the syntax of Hans's statement. First, his wish is directed more toward the future. I think this is a developmental step, facilitated by the analysis removing an obstacle to it.[4] Second, we may be hearing the beginnings of an identification with the father – "I want to be *like* you" – as a softening of the wish to replace him. The fantasy may be a solution to the negative oedipal conflicts as well; the bigger behind may be an effort to identify with his mother.

I have tried to show how little Hans's mode of thinking, appropriate for the oedipal phase, once repressed, could contribute to the formation of an adult neurosis. Freud's fidelity in reporting verbatim vignettes allows us to see in Hans's syntax how his capacity to anticipate the future, coupled with his egocentric theory of cause and effect, his largely unrepressed access to his sexual and aggressive urges, his egocentric misattribution of motives to others, and his confusion of thought and action creates his vulnerability and, to a large extent, dictates his symptomatic solution.

Notes

1   It is curious that the full title of the report is "The Analysis of a Phobia in a Five-Year-Old Boy," despite the fact that the report begins at age 3 and ends with the resolution of the phobia just as Hans turned five.
2   By way of illustration, note Freud's reasoning in the case history: "It was … increased affection for his mother which turned suddenly into anxiety – which, as we should say, succumbed to repression. We do not yet know from what quarter the impetus towards repression may have come …. Hans's anxiety, which thus corresponded to a repressed erotic longing" (Freud, 1909, p. 25).
3   Slap (1961, p. 259) comes to a similar conclusion.
4   I will not attempt to tackle the very important and complex question of how the analysis accomplished that. For one such effort, see Bierman (2007).

References

Abrams, S. (1984). Fantasy and reality in the oedipal phase – a conceptual overview. *The Psychoanalytic Study of the Child, 39*(1), 83–100.

Bierman, J.S. (2007). The psychoanalytic process in the treatment of Little Hans. *The Psychoanalytic Study of the Child. 62*(1), 92–110.

Blum, H.P. (2007). Little Hans. A contemporary overview. *The Psychoanalytic Study of the Child, 62*(1), 44–60.

Freud, A. (1963). The concept of developmental lines. *The Psychoanalytic Study of the Child, 18*(1), 245–65.

Freud, S. (1901). The psychopathology of everyday life. *SE* 6, 1–296.

Freud, S. (1909). Analysis of a phobia in a five-year-old boy. *SE* 10, 3–152.

Freud, S. (1923). The ego and the id. *SE* 19, 3–68.

Freud, S. (1926). Inhibitions, symptoms, and anxiety. *SE* 20, 77–178.

Neubauer, P.B. (2007). Exploring Little Hans. *The Psychoanalytic Study of the Child, 62*(1), 143–52.

Sandler, A.–M. (1975). Comments on the significance of Piaget's work for psychoanalysis. *International Review of Psycho-Analysis*, 2(4), 365–77.

Slap, J.W. (1961). Little Hans's tonsillectomy. *The Psychoanalytic Quarterly, 30*(4), 259–61.

Young-Bruehl, E. (2007). Little Hans in the history of child analysis. *The Psychoanalytic Study of the Child, 62*, 28–43.

Chapter 3

The Third Wish
Some Thoughts on Using Magic
Against Magic

My conclusion from the previous two chapters was that neurotic symptom-atology is based on the repression of a wish that is deemed *dangerous to be wished*. Given that the magical thinking (omnipotence of thought) appro-priate to the oedipal phase is also repressed, the wish *and the magical thinking that judges it to be dangerous* persist unconsciously in unmodified form. In what follows I describe one unexpected consequence of the oedipal syntax of magical thinking.

In the section on wish-fulfillment in dreams in *Introductory Lectures on Psycho-Analysis*, Freud (1915–1917) cites the following fairy tale:

> A good fairy promised a poor married couple to grant them the fulfill-ment of their first three wishes. They were delighted, and made up their minds to choose their three wishes carefully. But the smell of sausages being fried in the cottage next door tempted the woman to wish for a couple of them. They were there in a flash; and this was the first wish-fulfillment. But the man was furious, and in his rage wished that the sausages were hanging on his wife's nose. This happened too; and the sausages were not to be dislodged from their new position. This was the second wish-fulfillment; but the wish was the man's and its fulfill-ment was most disagreeable for his wife. You know the rest of the story. Since after all they were in fact one – man and wife – the third wish was bound to be that the sausages should come away from the woman's nose.
>
> (Freud, 1915–1917, p. 216)

In his subsequent discussion, Freud describes how the first wish was the woman's, directly fulfilled; the second was both the fulfillment of the husband's wish and the punishment of the wife for her foolishness. He then adds, in parentheses, "We shall discover in neuroses the motive for the third wish, the last remaining one in the fairy tale." The editor has appended a footnote to this parenthetical remark: "It is not clear what is intended here" (Freud, 1915–1917, p. 219; brackets omitted).

DOI: 10.4324/9781003360391-5

Although I cannot know Freud's intentions, I would like to suggest a motive for the third wish, which comes up in clinical work with some frequency: It is the unconscious conviction that the only cure for harmful magic is reparative magic. In what follows I would like to describe the dilemma of the person facing the third wish, as illustrated in literary examples, then use a brief vignette to try to capture the same transitional moment in the clinical situation. In doing so I will recall what I take to be Freud's solution, which was to exploit transference magic to combat neurotic magic.

Freud understood neurosis to be the outcome of a problematic resolution of the Oedipus complex involving the repression of a forbidden wish. The wish then remains unconsciously influential, but no longer subject to reality testing as a consequence of the repression. But we need to recall that what is repressed is not only the wish but also the mode of thinking involved at the time, including the belief in the magic of thoughts – a characteristic of the phallic-oedipal phase of development, during which the distinction between thinking and acting is not yet consolidated. It is thus that the neurotic subject is convinced that his wishes are so powerful as to be (literally) unthinkable, which is why repression is required in the first place.

The clinician who tries to bring reality to bear on the distinction between thought and action will sometimes encounter an unexpected obstacle: For some patients, the dawning awareness that their thoughts have no magical power implies that they must give up the only means they can imagine to undo the damage for which they blame themselves. The sense of this dilemma is captured very economically in the old joke retold by Woody Allen at the end of the movie *Annie Hall* (1977), in which a man tells a psychiatrist that his brother thinks he is a chicken. When the doctor advises bringing him in, the man declines because he needs the eggs.

The theme of using magic to undo misused magic is a common one in literature and folklore. W.-W. Jacobs's horror story "The Monkey's Paw" (1902) has the same "three wishes" structure as the fairy tale Freud cites: A wish for wealth causes the death of a loved one; a wish to bring him back threatens another horror; then the third wish must be used to undo the damage and return to the *status quo ante*. Goethe's poem "The Sorcerer's Apprentice" (1797) offers us a version that should encourage analysts: The apprentice appropriates his absent master's wand and wreaks havoc he cannot control. When the sorcerer returns, he uses his stronger magic to put things right.

In a recent contribution, Friedman (2008) referred to the "riddle of psychoanalysis, which is that its theory seems best suited to explain why psychoanalytic treatment won't work" (p. 1105). He was referring, of course, to the powerful attachment patients have to their neurotic solutions. The version of that problem I am concerned with here is the reluctance to give up magical protection from magical dangers. Whitebook (2002) makes a compelling case for the role of magic in analysis – specifically, the magic invested in the analyst in the transference. He argued that Freud was unwilling to acknowledge the use of transference magic – suggestion – in the analyst's functioning: "The claim [Freud] now [1916–1917] put forward was that psychoanalysis doesn't indulge or manipulate the transference, but analyzes and dissolves it" (Whitebook, 2002, p. 1202).

My reading of Freud leads me to a different conclusion. Freud repeatedly addressed the technical problem of overcoming the patient's motivation to avoid change, in ways that make clear that he was aware of the exploitation of the patient's belief in magic – specifically parental magic in the transference. In the same year in which he introduced the "repudiation of suggestion as a litmus test to distinguish "true psycho-analysis" from hypnotism – and, indeed, from all other forms of nonanalytic therapy" (Whitebook, 2002, p. 1201) – Freud wrote that "we take care of the patient's final independence by employing suggestion in order to get him to accomplish a piece of psychical work" (1912, p. 106).

In subsequent work, Freud went on to say, "Our hope is to achieve [the overcoming of resistances] by exploiting the patient's transference to the person of the physician, so as to induce him to adopt our conviction of the inexpediency of the repressive process established in childhood" (1919, p. 159). Freud's controversial unilateral decision to terminate the treatment of the Wolf Man involved a related idea: "I was obliged to wait until his attachment to myself had become strong enough to counterbalance this shrinking [from a self-sufficient existence], and then played off this one factor against the other" (1918, p. 11). Freud's notion of an "unobjectionable" positive transference, which he describes as "the vehicle of success in psychoanalysis exactly as it is in other methods of treatment" (1912, p. 105), is a further example of the same idea.[1]

In a summary of changes of aims in psychoanalytic technique, Freud (1920) wrote that the task became "pointing [the resistances] out to the patient and inducing him by human influence – this was where suggestion operating as 'transference' played its part – to abandon the resistances" (p. 18). In a footnote a few pages later (added in 1923), he commented:

> I have argued elsewhere … that what thus comes to the help of the compulsion to repeat is the factor of "suggestion" in the treatment – that is, the patient's submission to the physician, which has its roots deep in his unconscious parental complex.
>
> (Freud, 1920, p. 20, footnote)

It is true that Freud also distinguished analysis from other therapies by the ultimate analysis of the transference:

> In every other kind of suggestive treatment the transference is carefully preserved and left untouched; in analysis it is itself subjected to treatment

> and is dissected in all the shapes in which it appears. At the end of an ana-
> lytic treatment the transference must itself be cleared away.
>
> (Freud, 1915–1917, p. 453)

Whether or not one envisions the transference as ultimately being "cleared away," it seems that Freud accepted the need to use the power of the positive transference along the way to counteract the patient's attachment to the neurosis. As I read him, Freud was not denying transference magic; rather, he saw it as a necessary step, not specific to analysis, that will subsequently be addressed analytically, i.e., made the subject of analysis.

We are concerned here with one aspect of the neurotic *status quo* – namely, the patient's unconscious belief in the magical power of thought. In the clinical situation, one makes it safer for the patient to relinquish his magic by (temporarily) allowing the patient to believe and elaborate the belief that the analyst, *in loco parentis*, has magic that is even more powerful. A common clinical moment may illustrate the magic-versus-magic dilemma.

In the third year of his analysis, a generally inhibited man, Mr. M, began an hour with a typically dismissive remark about the "couch talk" he was about to engage in (rather than exercising his preference for having a formal agenda). He then reported a pattern he had seen in his own behavior: He would become restless in his marriage and then enjoy a daydream about an anonymous sexual encounter in which he exercised his dominance. Mr. M noticed that, after the daydream, he would latch onto some trivial event and take it as evidence that he was physically impaired or endangered – for example, stepping in a puddle would lead to an obsession about getting infected, or a mark on his skin would provoke a worry about melanoma.

As we discussed the sequence, one of its meanings became clear: In each case, the last step in the daydream was the idea that Mr. M would not survive without his wife to take care of him. As the inhibiting function of the illness daydream became clearer, the sexual fantasy that began the sequence became more accessible. The patient became more anxious as his dissatisfactions with his wife began to emerge, and he tried to find ways to take the subject off the table. I told him that he treated his thoughts as if they were acts. Finally, Mr. M said, "I may be unhappy in my marriage, but I can't think about it, because then I'll have to leave her."

I responded, "You're saying that if you have a choice you won't have a choice."

I would imagine the full meaning of the patient's statement in the clinical context to be something like this: "I believe that, by not thinking about wanting to leave my wife, I am preventing my thoughts from making it happen. I have put myself in your hands because I believe you have the power to protect me, and so I can reluctantly accept your suggestion to take the first step and begin to entertain the idea that I have no such magic. That takes me to the next step: If I face my feelings about my wife, I would then think about leaving her, and then I would have no magical power to resist the magical power of that thought."

The analyst's transference magic is the power of the father who can open the closet door to reveal that there is no monster hiding behind it, only because the child trusts that the father has the strength of the monster. In the clinical moment described above, Mr. M is in a transitional position akin to the child who trusts the father enough to let him open the closet, even though he still believes in the monster inside.

At another point in the analysis, in the context of "unobjectionable" transference love, Mr. M told me: "I'm trying to program myself to be less robotic." At that point, it would seem that he was trying to change – but he still needed the eggs.

By the end of a successful analysis, the patient's realization that the analyst has no magic is both a disappointment and a liberation; no longer dependent on a magical solution, the patient is freed to seek the eggs where he can actually get them. Like the man behind the curtain in *The Wizard of Oz* (Fleming, 1939), the analyst is reduced to human proportions. In Oz, Dorothy is upset; she tells the wizard he is a bad man. The wizard objects, saying he is a good man but a bad wizard. Therapists could do worse than strive for the ideal of being good people and bad wizards.

Note

1 Whitebook (2002) cites this as the "one important exception" to Freud's disavowal of suggestion (p. 1202).

References

Allen, W. (Director). (1977). *Annie Hall* [Film]. United Artists.

Fleming, V. (Director). (1939). *The Wizard of Oz* [Film]. Metro-Goldwyn-Mayer.

Freud, S. (1912). The dynamics of transference. SE *12*, 97–108.

Freud, S. (1915–1917). Introductory lectures on psycho-analysis. SE *15–16*.

Freud, S. (1918). From the history of an infantile neurosis ("the Wolf-Man"). SE *17*, 3–124.

Freud, S. (1919). Lines of advance in psycho-analytic therapy. SE *17*, 157–68.

Freud, S. (1920). Beyond the pleasure principle. SE *18*, 3–64.

Friedman, L. (2008). Loewald. *Journal of the American Psychoanalytic Association, 56,* 1105–15.

Goethe, J.W. (1797). The sorcerer's apprentice (E. Zeydel, Trans.). www.reelyredd. com/1006sorcerersapprentice.htm

Jacobs, W.W. (1902). *The monkey's paw: A story in three scenes* (dramatized by L. N. Parker). Samuel French (1910).

Whitebook, J. (2002). Slow magic. *Journal of the American Psychoanalytic Association, 50,* 1197–1217.

Chapter 4

Perverse Syntax and the Perverse Attitude Toward Reality

In this chapter I shift away from those people whose suffering is a consequence of the successful use of repression and turn to another broad category.
Jacob Arlow (1971) coined the term "character perversion" to emphasize the
relationship between certain character traits and the defenses used in certain
sexual perversions. It has been my experience that these same traits occur in
women as well as in men (Grossman, 1992). These patients seem to share an
attitude toward reality, a willingness to alter its status in order to avoid anxiety or depressive affect. Arlow's description opens the door to a fuller consideration of "perverse" thinking in a vast group of people who do not necessarily
have compulsory sexual perversions. In the next two chapters, I will try to
put together a picture of the perverse attitude toward reality and examine the
syntax of thought that defines it.

A probation officer in analysis was troubled by his frequent thoughts about
molesting young girls. On one occasion, he intentionally brushed against the
buttocks of a teenage girl in his charge, after the thought "came to him" that
he would like to do so. He understood the episode as evidence that, because
he could not prevent the thought, he acted on it – in effect, the thought made
him do it. His analyst pointed out that he talked about the thought as if it
were not him doing the thinking. He agreed; he had just "received" it.

After some discussion of the uses to which he put this claim of passivity
with respect to his thinking, the analyst wondered what had been left out
of the account. How was it that the only thought he had attended to at the
time was the wishful one? His analyst suggested that he might not have let
himself become aware of *all* his thoughts at the time. The patient confirmed
that he had had another thought about getting in trouble, but he had "turned
down the volume on reality." He allowed himself the gratification of a
forbidden wish by finding a way to disavow the troublesome reality of the possible consequences of his action. He knew about it, but it was not so "loud"
that he had to treat it as important.[1]

This is a simple example of two defensive maneuvers that are aimed at two
different targets. The patient's insistence on his passivity was directed against

DOI: 10.4324/9781003360391-6

his forbidden wish: He did not "want" to act, he was "compelled" to do so by an "intrusive" thought. His "turning down the volume on reality" was directed against a troubling perception of reality (an idea of the consequences), rather than against the impulse. Freud (1940a, p. 204) tentatively distinguished between the defensive operations in neurosis and those in perversion on this basis: In neurosis, the wish is renounced, disguised, or otherwise inhibited, out of respect for dangers perceived in reality; whereas in perversion, the perception of reality is altered and the wish retained. Although Freud was careful to note that this distinction was not absolute, I believe it has broad utility in everyday clinical work: It gives us a basis to define a class of phenomena that has in common the defensive alteration of the sense of reality.

Although the phenomena that comprise this class are quite varied, their common effect upon reality makes them similar in one clinically important respect: When unpleasurable affect threatens, reality no longer has its compelling quality. Broadly put, this accounts for the difficulty in treating the perverse patient; and this difficulty is shared, in varying degree, by the other phenomena in the class. Included in this class are perversions, "character perversion," "fetish equivalents" (Calef et al., 1980), some compulsions, e.g., kleptomania (Zavitzianos, 1971), "negation as a character trait" (Weinshel, 1977), depersonalization and derealization (Freud, 1936; Arlow, 1966; Renik, 1978), confusing dream and reality (Calef, 1972), and others.

I would like to survey some of these entities briefly, in order to consider the kind of thinking involved in all of them, and then offer a clinical example to consider the challenges to treatment such cases present. Finally, I will comment on the role of the superego in the type of defensive maneuvers under discussion.

In his discussion of the "unrealistic character," Arlow (1971) drew the connection between the trait described and its origins in voyeurism and fetishism, in which the perception of the penisless female genital stirs up such intense castration anxiety that the reality of the perception has to be disavowed, or attention has to be focused intensively on a peripheral detail, away from the disturbing aspect of the perception. The detail, the fetish, serves as a representation of the female penis and negates the disturbing perception. As Arlow put it, "The voyeur is compelled to look but not to see" (1971, p. 322); he is not compelled to accept what he sees as important. The fetishist finds something else to look at in order to distract his attention from what is disturbing.

Arlow described two other related character traits under the heading of character perversion. One is the petty liar, who reassures himself that if he can obscure the truth from others, he need not face the truth himself. Arlow noted that the lie is a fetish equivalent, a "screen percept" (1971, p. 326). But it also discredits the truth, as if to say it may just as well be a lie. The other trait can be seen in the practical joker, who inspires anxiety in others and then takes

pleasure in exposing the hoax. Arlow observed the similarity of this trait to
the defenses of the transvestite (1971, p. 326), in which the perverse activity
implies that femaleness (i.e., penislessness) is only an appearance.

Character perversion is not uncommon, but it escapes notice because the
disturbance is relatively mild and the patient does not complain of it (Arlow,
1971, p. 318). Arlow restricted his discussion to male patients, but character
perversion occurs in women as well (Grossman, 1992).

Greenacre (1955) identified "forms of fetishism which are not always
clearly linked to the genital functioning (such as certain drug addictions,
kleptomanias, special religious practices, the use of lucky charms) ... [which]
seem to occur in the female as well as the male" (p. 59, footnote). These and
other related clinical phenomena are sometimes labeled "fetish equivalents."
In other words, they share the defensive practices with frank sexual fetishism,
even though they have different aims. Zavitzianos (1971) referred to kleptomania as "the female fetishism" (p. 303) and noted in passing that there are
similarities between perversion and psychopathy (p. 304) – suggesting the
importance of superego functioning in the disorder.

Calef et al. (1980) considered enuresis as the "functional equivalent of
a fetish." In the case they described, the patient "experienced the analysis
as a dream from which he did not wish to be awakened ... [R]eality [was]
discounted as unreal, ... unimportant, even non-existent" (p. 295). Note
that the clinical problem was that the patient took the same liberties with
unpleasant treatment realities as he did with other threatening perceptions.

Weinshel (1977) has studied a variety of nonpsychotic patients with focal
defects of reality sense. Under the heading of "negation as a character trait,"
he described a woman who protected herself from disturbing reality by a variety of actions that conveyed the sense of "I didn't mean it" (Weinshel, 1977).
In another contribution, Weinshel (1986) reported the perceptual distortions
of three neurotic women in analysis who, at stressful moments, transiently
gave up their reality testing capacity in favor of unrealistic illusions.

Arlow (1966) described the "dissociation of the function of the observing
self from the experiencing self" in hysterical hallucinosis, which he saw as the
opposite of depersonalization. In the former, "there is maximal investment in
the function of immediate experience and an almost complete obliteration of
the function of self observation." In the latter, "self awareness is heightened
and the sense of participation in action is minimized or alienated" (Arlow,
1966, p. 463).

Calef's (1972) case of a patient who insisted on the reality of his dream,
and disavowed the reality of his waking life, is a fascinating counterpart to
Freud's (1940a) case, mentioned in passing, of a paranoid man whose dreams
accurately represented reality that was denied in waking thought (Freud,
1940a, p. 202). Calef's patient complained of insomnia, until they discovered
that the patient was dreaming that he was awake. Renik (1978) discussed

the role of the restriction of attention with respect to certain perceptions in depersonalization.

Freud (1923) described how little boys disavow their perceptions of the female genital and "believe that they *do* see a penis, all the same. They gloss over the contradiction between observation and preconception by telling themselves that the penis is still small and will grow bigger" (pp. 143–4). In his next contribution, Freud considered the position of the ego with respect to conflict with either the id or external reality. He wrote:

> It will be possible for the ego to avoid a rupture in any direction by deforming itself, by submitting to encroachments on its own unity and even perhaps by effecting a cleavage or division of itself. In this way the inconsistencies, eccentricities and follies of men would appear *in a similar light* to their sexual perversions, through the acceptance of which they spare themselves repressions.
>
> (Freud, 1924, pp. 152–3; italics added)

Note that this "cleavage" is *similar to* (i.e., shared with, but not limited to) the perversions and is an alternative to repression.

Freud described the conditions for this type of thinking as a "split in the ego" (1927, 1936, 1940a, 1940b). In his paper "Fetishism" (1927), he discussed the simultaneous holding of the belief that women have penises and the knowledge that they do not (p. 154). But in the same paper, he described the same process in an obsessional patient without a fetish, with respect to the disavowal of his father's death: "The attitude which fitted in with the wish [that his father were still alive] and the attitude which fitted in with the reality existed side by side" (Freud, 1927, p. 156).

Although Freud found that fetishism provided a particularly fruitful opportunity to study the splitting of the ego, he did not consider the disavowal on which it is based to be limited to it (Freud, 1940a, pp. 203–4). In a discussion of derealization, Freud (1936) described the situation in which the testimony of the senses is disavowed (p. 244); the perception coexists with the judgment that it is unreal. He likened the phenomenon to *déjà vu*. He told the story of the king who kills the bearer of bad news: The king "determines to treat the news as *non arrivé*" (Freud, 1936, p. 246).

Disavowal, which Freud links to the splitting of the ego, is one of a class of defensive maneuvers by which an intolerable reality is made bearable. By disavowal, I understand the stripping of disturbing meaning or consequence from a perception, without altering the perception itself. Related efforts to cope with intolerable perceptions include the distraction of attention from the disturbing percept and the illusory distortion of perception (as in Weinshel's [1986] cases). Note that fetishism involves both disavowal of the perception of a penisless genital and distraction from it by attending to the fetish object.

Disavowal, distraction, and illusion are defensive maneuvers directed against a threatening *perception*, which remains available to consciousness in some form. To say that a "split in the ego" is involved, as Freud does with respect to disavowal, is to say that the person is adept at keeping two apparently contradictory ideas in mind, without feeling the obligation to reconcile the two (Freud, 1940a, p. 203). The perception is available, but it does not have the evidentiary value to influence the cherished belief. It is precisely this facility, which I am calling the perverse attitude toward reality, that creates technical problems, about which I will have more to say later. Such patients can distinguish reality from fantasy, but, when it suits them not to, they do not find reality compelling.

Of course, the distinction between neurotic and perverse attitudes is not so hard and fast in practice. Every neurotic defense alters the perception of reality in some sense. Most obviously, the repression of a wish alters one's conscious self-perception, as well as one's understanding of conditions in the world as a consequence. Perceptions (and "reality") are never passively received "objective" facts, but constructions.

Furthermore, everyone uses both neurotic and perverse approaches in some mixture. But the attitude I am describing amounts to avoiding reality *as perceived*. It makes a substantial difference in working with a clinical phenomenon, whether we understand the mechanism involved as an effort to disguise or renounce a wish for fear of perceived consequences or as an effort to evade the implications of what is perceived. In the latter case, the degree of license to disavow, alter, or ignore what is in front of one's eyes has far-reaching consequences for treatment.

Examples of these phenomena are commonplace in every practice: My introductory vignette is a case in point. Another common version of taking these liberties with reality can be seen in the patient who tells a dream in such a way that the analyst always has to struggle to distinguish when the patient has stopped talking about the dream and begun to talk about reality — a distinction that does not seem to concern the patient.

A less common, if more striking, example also came up in work with dreams:

> A man in analysis began a Monday hour announcing that he had "that dream again" Sunday night. "It's funny; I never dream, as you well know. But I've had this identical dream twice before: I drive my car into the garage and leave it there. While walking, I witness an accident — puddles of blood. It is the corner of Nimitz and St. Andrew streets. The driver couldn't control the car."

The man was most impressed by the fact that he had had the same dream twice before. I was most impressed by the fact that he was talking as if I had heard it before, which I had not. He was certain that he had told me the dream twice before. In fact, he knew which days: He had the dream Wednesday and Friday mornings and reported it in his Wednesday and Friday hours.

At this point I reminded him that we had not met on Friday; he had not shown up. He was puzzled for a moment, but then he realized that, while driving to the hour, he had skidded on a slick patch of road and spun out into a ditch on St. Andrew Street. He then recalled that, on Wednesday, he had been driving on the Nimitz Freeway and had blown a front tire; he had struggled to control the car and pull over safely.

He described the accident on Friday. During the skid, he had felt as if he was in a dream. Immediately upon getting out of the car, he found that he was surveying the damage coolly, "as if I wasn't there." He remembered thinking calmly, "it never happened." In fact, he had gone home and thought no more about the accident, or about the hour he had been heading for.

The phrase "it never happened" reminded him of an incident from adolescence. It had been his habit to go to a certain bookstore, where he would look at sexually stimulating magazines while trying not to be conspicuous. Often he would get an erection, which he would "try to control." On the occasion he now recalled, he ejaculated. Immediately he felt as if he were in a dream, and he found himself thinking, "it never happened." As might be expected, he could not say whether this had happened more than once; indeed, even as he described the memory, he found himself wondering whether he had just dreamed it all in the first place.

He wondered about the dream. The car seemed important to him; in fact, he had been thinking about the dreams (*sic*) as "driving dreams." As he thought about the accident, he did not recall having experienced any fear that he might have been injured; instead, as it was happening, he had worried about damaging the car. "But," he said, "I suppose the car is an extension of myself." He recognized the allusion to his penis in the words but repeated that he had felt no danger.

The "accident" in the dream reminded him that his mother used to call it an "accident" when he wet the bed as a child, which he had done well into latency. She would joke that she had seen an elephant or some other animal come into his room in the night and wet his bed. He would recall waking to find he was "in a puddle," with no idea what had happened; apparently, he was often confused about whether it was a dream. Sometimes he would convince himself that he had seen the elephant – "witnessed the accident."

The patient was an only child whose father left his mother and him when he was three. The divorce left the mother impoverished and forced the two of them into a small apartment in which privacy was compromised. It seems that when mother would have a man spend the night, the child was exposed to their sexual activity – which the mother would subsequently deny, insisting that the child had been dreaming. His masturbation was another occasion for a collusion that "it never happened"; she tacitly agreed not to notice it, and he found a way to detach himself from it, as if it were not him doing it.

This example demonstrates an array of defensive operations, both "neurotic" and "perverse." To focus on the latter: His *déjà raconté*, depersonalization, derealization, confusion of dream and reality – all represent ways of discrediting troublesome perceptions of reality that allow him to gratify certain wishes in relatively unmodified form. What the patient did with the dream itself is a prime example: He treated it as a reality, and he treated the reality to which it alluded as a dream. The dream wish might be expressed as "I wasn't driving; it was only a dream."

There is nothing very unusual about taking reassurance from a dream in that form. Freud (1900) described a similar process in his discussion of examination dreams (pp. 273–6). Renik (1981) pointed out the reassurance in so-called typical anxiety dreams and superego dreams along these lines as well. What is more unusual is what the patient did *while awake*. He did not merely make a claim in his dream; he continued to make it in waking life. His conviction of already having told me about the "dreams" was a falsification, an enactment of a fantasy, which supported another disavowal in which he told himself he had merely dreamed the events.

Taking these liberties with reality helped him to keep the threatening preconscious perception of the accident away from the center of his awareness. Note that he did not *forget* the accident or the hours he missed; he had them in mind, but they had lost the force of reality – they were treated as if they were a dream, whereas his daydreamed version was treated as reality.

This example may seem cause for optimism. After all, the patient seemed to discover and reveal a good deal about his castration anxiety; he seemed to have recovered some key memories, all in one dramatic hour. But (as my patient constantly reassured himself) appearances are deceiving. The fate of this material, and much like it, was to be doubted, altered, discounted as an interesting fiction, blurred out of existence or ignored, as we continued in our work. The hour might as well never have taken place. His conscience, heir to the interactions with his parents, did not compel him to accept the testimony of his senses when those perceptions threatened him. To the contrary, he was more than willing to give up his frightening perceptions as if they were bad dreams.

The Role of the Superego

I am following a line of thought suggested by Calef (1972) and others in conceiving of this liberty with respect to the demands of reality as a compromise of a function of the superego. Calef raised the question of the "relationship between the functions of conscience and the kind of conviction necessary to be achieved through analytic work" (1972, p. 169, footnote). He and his co-workers also suggested that the "clinical observations of the reversals of fantasy and reality" – the way reality was disavowed in his case report – provided a "clue ... as to how the superego functions or fails to do so in reality testing and in the vicissitudes of conviction" (Calef et al., 1980, p. 295, footnote).

From the standpoint of analytic work, this aspect of the functioning of conscience is crucial: Does the patient have the honesty to face a disturbing perception of reality sufficiently to consider it, or does reality lose its status when it is perceived as threatening? Arlow (1971) described a "superego subverted by anxiety" (p. 333). I have suggested (Grossman, 1992) that the need to escape depressive affect may have similar effects on the functioning of conscience. In my example above, as in Arlow's (1980) discussion, it was possible to infer the role played in superego formation by identification with corrupt aspects of the parents' ways of handling disturbing reality. Weinshel's (1986) study of perceptual distortions also noted the contribution to his patients' superego functioning by the parents, who had been "egregiously unconcerned about respect for reality and reality testing" (p. 363).

It is worth stressing that the "subversion" of the superego is relative and variable. For instance, Weinshel (1986) noted that, in each of the cases he reported, the patient felt that she was doing something wrong; they all realized that "rejecting a realistic appraisal of reality was contrary to the precepts of their own conscience" (p. 363). The man in my example had fewer such misgivings.

Clinical Considerations

The clinical significance of this distinction is that it makes it possible to anticipate certain difficulties in treatment. To the extent that patients have the liberty to discount the consequences of what they perceive, they will be able to evade threatening perceptions (including self-perceptions) in the analysis on which the reconsideration of their experiences depends.

In practice, this means that apparent gains of insight, insofar as they threaten certain wished-for gratifications, may evaporate. The patient may recall the words but discount the significance. The whole treatment may take on an "as if" quality, as ideas are stripped of their consequence in reality. At the same time, fantasies are treated as fact; the patient may admit that "really" she knows something is not the case but insists on acting as if it were. This applies most dramatically to the relationship to the analyst, which is treated as simply real. It is not uncommon for the analyst to become a fetish (Renik, 1992).

This has implications for clinical work in two respects. First, analytic attention to these operations commands precedence. Not much can be accomplished if the patient discounts the significance of every disturbing fact before her until the discounting itself is made the subject of the work.

Second, access to understanding these types of liberties with reality often will require the analyst to take a stand with respect to the demands of reality – not as the authority on its nature, but as the advocate of giving reality its due. I believe therapists do so routinely in small ways in every treatment, although it is not always so conceived. My reminding my patient that we had not met on certain days is a simple example. It follows from the perverse attitude toward reality that aspects of the analytic situation that *encourage* the patient to blur the distinction between fantasy and reality stand to make things worse. For example, the recumbent position on the couch with the analyst out of sight invites the patient to treat the analysis as if it were unreal.

In the extreme, the analyst may have to be the unilateral spokesperson for reality. For example, a man in analysis found himself in the position of having his job eliminated. Another job was available to him, but it would require moving to another town. Gradually, it became clear that he was continuing to act as if the analysis could go on indefinitely. The analyst pointed out his doing so, and the patient talked freely of his wish that he would never have to leave. But despite this apparent awareness, the patient continued to live his life as if there were no imminent threat. Although money was running out, he made no plans to move. He had not made the steps necessary to take the new job. He paid no attention to the impending interruption of analysis.

This situation persisted for some time, with the analyst calling attention to these maneuvers as he recognized them. Much of the fantasy was elaborated: that the analyst would see the patient for free or even support him; that the analyst would intervene in magical ways to preserve the relationship, and so on. Hostile and aggressive meanings were also considered. The patient was willing to consider his "fantasy," but with the hidden stipulation that the painful reality was also to be considered a fantasy, with no other status.

Finally, the analyst told the patient that it was clear they would not be able to continue past a certain date, and that he (the patient) needed to make plans accordingly. The patient found this a rude shock at first. He felt the analyst had no right to "take [his] fantasies away." He described it as the analyst waking him up. This led to more conviction about the power of his fantasies, especially with respect to the analyst's power to bestow and withdraw special gifts. It also led to more awareness of the facility with which he neglected troublesome realities, and something of the history of his experiences of "rude awakenings" and his way of coping with them by telling himself he was dreaming. He also began to make his moving plans.

Discussion

The phenomena described in this chapter are common examples of a suspension of the functions of conscience with respect to the obligations of reality testing. A troublesome perception may be treated as a dream, as a movie, as a joke, or as a trivial matter. It is not obliterated; it is available to consciousness in some form. But it is stipulated, acknowledged for the record, stripped of significance, altered, and/or ignored. Taking such liberties with reality requires the collusion of conscience.

The various phenomena considered in this investigation are more closely allied to perverse than to neurotic processes, in that they involve an attempt to alter the perception of a threatening or painful reality rather than renounce or disguise the wish that stirs up the expectation of punishment. These maneuvers occur in men and women; they may be motivated by anxiety or by depressive affect (see Grossman, 1992).

Defensive operations aimed at reality are not always obvious; we tend to assume that certain obstacles have been surmounted, certain gains have been consolidated, when they seem to make sense to the patient and they make sense to us. Sometimes the first suspicion that the patient is taking certain liberties with reality is the realization that the patient is not using her apparent discoveries in her daily life; instead, she is restricting her "insights" to the analytic hour.

The analyst's awareness of these varieties of disavowal will not make them disappear; after all, the ego and superego functions that are compromised are just those that are needed to collaborate fully in the analytic work. But it can make a difficult treatment situation somewhat more manageable if the disavowals can be made the subject of the work. The analyst's ability to anticipate such difficulties will make it easier to call the patient's attention to the various ways she negotiates troublesome perceptions. But the analyst must also be prepared to speak for the demands of reality when the patient refuses to credit it.

Note

1   I am indebted to Dr. Janis Baeuerlen for this example.

References

Arlow, J.A. (1966). Depersonalization and derealization. In R.M. Loewenstein et al. (Eds.), *Psychoanalysis. A general psychology. Essays in honor of Heinz Hartmann* (pp. 456–78). International Universities Press.

Arlow, J.A. (1971). Character perversion. In I.W. Marcus (Ed.), *Currents in psychoanalysis* (pp. 317–36). International Universities Press.

Arlow, J.A. (1980). The revenge motive in the primal scene. *Journal of the American Psychoanalytic Association, 28*(3), 519–42.

Calef, V. (1972). "I am awake": Insomnia or dream? An addendum to the forgetting of dreams. *The Psychoanalytic Quarterly, 41*(2), 161–71.

Calef, V., Weinshel, E.M., Renik, O., & Mayer, E.L. (1980). Enuresis: A functional equivalent of a fetish. *International Journal of Psychoanalysis, 61*, 295–305.

Freud, S. (1900). *The interpretation of dreams.* SE 4–5.

Freud, S. (1923) The infantile genital organization: An interpolation into the theory of sexuality SE *19*, 141–8.

Freud, S. (1924). Neurosis and psychosis. SE *19*, 149–56.

Freud, S. (1927) Fetishism SE *21*, 149–58.

Freud, S. (1936). A disturbance of memory on the Acropolis. SE *22*, 239–50.

Freud, S. (1940a). An outline of psycho-analysis. SE *23*, 141–208.

Freud, S. (1940b). Splitting of the ego in the process of defense. SE *23*, 271–8.

Greenacre, P. (1955). *Emotional growth. Psychoanalytic studies of the gifted and a great variety of other individuals* (Vol. 1). International Universities Press (1971).

Grossman, L. (1992). An example of "character perversion" in a woman. *The Psychoanalytic Quarterly, 61*, 581–9.

Renik, O. (1978). The role of attention in depersonalization. *The Psychoanalytic Quarterly, 47*(4), 588–605.

Renik, O. (1981). Typical examination dreams, "superego dreams," and traumatic dreams. *The Psychoanalytic Quarterly, 50*(2), 159–89.

Renik, O. (1992). Use of the analyst as a fetish. *The Psychoanalytic Quarterly, 61*(4), 542–63.

Weinshel, E.M. (1977). "I didn't mean it." Negation as a character trait. *The Psychoanalytic Study of the Child, 32*(1), 387–419.

Weinshel, E.M. (1986). Perceptual distortions during analysis: Some observations on the role of the superego in reality testing. In A.D. Richards & M.S. Willick (Eds.), *Psychoanalysis. The Science of mental conflict. Essays in honor of Charles Brenner* (pp. 353–376). Analytic Press.

Zavitzianos, G. (1971). Fetishism and exhibitionism in the female and their relationship to psychopathy and kleptomania. *The International Journal of Psychoanalysis, 52*(3), 297–305.

Chapter 5

Reality Testing in Perverse Organization

> *You're saying it's a falsehood ... and Sean Spicer, our press secretary, gave alternative facts to that.*
>
> (Kellyanne Conway)

In the last chapter I described the syntax of perverse thought. Simply put, it is wishful thinking, and it seems to involve a problem with delaying gratification. It takes the syntactical form *if I want it so much, I can't not have it*, and *if it scares me so much, it can't be real*. I have described many clinical manifestations already. Here I might add that perversely organized patients rarely feel a *little* anxious. They either feel no anxiety or they are overcome by panic or depressive feelings. In contrast to neurotics, they do not use anxiety as an effective warning signal. I believe that to be another consequence of an ineffective repression barrier.

But I called the last chapter "the perverse attitude toward reality." So maybe it would make more sense for this category to be defined not by the syntax of perverse thought, but by a characteristic perverse ontology – that is, a theory of what is real. The syntax reveals the ontology. In the Marx brothers' movie *Animal Crackers*, when Chico's character is caught in the act of transgressing, he asks the witnesses to choose between believing him or their own eyes. The humor of 1930 has become the politics of the 21st century, with its "alternative facts"; both reflect the perverse ontology that reality is pliable according to one's wishes.

It is not a new idea to identify differing ontologies with different psychic organizations – although I think it is an underappreciated one. Loewald (1952) pointed out that Freud's view of the environment as constantly hostile and threatening to the human organism was an obsessional neurotic's ontology. Our language gives us the means to bridge the gap between our individual worlds – but it also helps us maintain an *illusion* of a shared world by concealing those differences (see Chapter 10).

Perverse people, by virtue of maintaining a split between the world as they "concede" it to be and the world as they want it to be, seem to take two

DOI: 10.4324/9781003360391-7

contradictory ontological positions. But they live in the wishful-thinking world – and so we may infer that their actual ontology is that they get to choose what is real. In this chapter I will take up how they manage to do that.

Psychic Reality

The term *psychic reality* was introduced by Freud in 1900 (p. 613) (see Arlow, 1985) to emphasize that the motivational power of unconscious fantasy in neurosis was at least as great as the power of reality. That discovery enabled us to understand the "unrealistic" convictions and paradoxical behaviors with which our patients struggle. As our understanding of the power of unconscious fantasy has grown, so has our emphasis on its role in treatment. In some cases, we may be tempted to forget that "psychic reality" is *fantasy*.

Taken literally, the term "psychic reality" is both redundant and misleading. It is redundant because all reality is "psychic"; perception is not a passive act of reception and recording but an active process of selection and interpretation. "Material" or "external" reality, terms that seem to convey a sense of a reality independent of perception, are no less the creation of perceptual and interpretive acts, but they refer to a consensus or at least a serviceable overlap of our individual perceptions. The term is misleading because what we mean by "psychic reality" is not some kind of "reality," but enduring unconscious fantasy. If we use the term to emphasize how influential unconscious or untested fantasy can be, it is a useful if imprecise concept. But its misleading connotations – that it is an alternative to an apprehensible "objective" reality, and that "psychic reality" is somehow on a par with tested reality – create a certain potential for clinical difficulties.

I will try to describe some of those difficulties as they arise in work with perverse patients. In order to do so, I will offer my view of what is meant by reality testing. I will argue that, in such patients, the crucial distinction is not between their "psychic" and "material" realities, but between their tested reality and untested fantasy. I will suggest that, if the concept of "psychic reality" elevates fantasy to the status of an alternative "reality" in the mind of the analyst, the outcome may be collusion with the patient's characterological blurring of the distinction between fantasy and reality.

In patients whose capacity to "test reality" is well established, bringing a fantasy to light may be all that is required to set the process of change in motion; the patient will recognize the fantasy as such soon after it is made explicit. But as I described in the previous chapter, perverse patients insist that "psychic reality" is just as real as tested reality. In such cases, the analytic task is not so much to discover and appreciate the patient's "psychic reality," but to demonstrate how and why the patient is actively confusing reality with fantasy. In work with such patients, thinking of "psychic reality" as a "kind" of reality may lead inadvertently to reinforcing the avoidance of distinguishing fantasy from reality, i.e., the abrogation of reality testing.

Reality and Reality Testing

From the point of view of mundane experience, perhaps the most curious thing about reality is that we have a name for it at all. One would think it would be transparent and taken for granted. As Marshall McLuhan (Levenson, 1988) observed, we do not know who discovered water, but we do know it was not a fish. We might amend that view if we consider what would make it easier for a fish to discover water: The discoverer would have to have been a fish out of water. How does one "discover" (i.e., create a concept of) reality? We must surmise that it happens by contrast; that is, that one first experiences the failure of one's expectations. A distinction is thus born where one was unnecessary before between the expected and the actual, i.e., between the real and the imaginary. The function of a concept of reality is to distinguish it from fantasy.

In our field, we deal as much in fantasy as in reality. Our developmental studies and clinical experience teach us that there is a crucial stretch of childhood in which our perceptions have become very organized and sophisticated, but our capacity to distinguish thoughts from actions, wishes from deeds, "inner" from "outer" – the capacity to test reality – is not yet firmly established (Chapters 1 and 2). Ideas actively sequestered from awareness are not subject to reality testing, so fantastic ideas persist and remain influential. Various schools of psychoanalysis have differing ideas about the timing or about the typical content of sequestered ideas, but the principle of this critical confluence of developmental events is familiar to all analysts.

Throughout life, we fantasize without becoming aware of doing so; we dream or daydream constantly. When the occasion arises for us to shift our attention to this constantly active "primary process" that underlies all mentation – for example, by attempting to free-associate – we can make a judgment about the reality of our imagining. But for the most part, we do not notice the constant activity of our imagination.

As a commonplace example: One morning, at a time when I was on a strict diet, I awoke with a feeling of shame and irritation with myself for having succumbed to the temptation to eat some forbidden food. I felt annoyed with myself all day, until someone happened to ask me how the diet was going. When I thought about it, I realized I had not gone off the diet; I had dreamed the lapse, and by refraining from asking myself any questions about the reality of the event – that is, by not "testing reality" – I had preserved the illicit satisfaction of the dream snack.

Thanks to Freud's noticing the activity of *his* imagination, we have come to learn that certain powerfully held fantasies are actively kept out of awareness because (as part of the fantasy) awareness of them is too threatening. But avoiding the threat of awareness also prevents putting the fantastic ideas to the test. The fateful consequence of those actions is that the fantasy retains all the power of belief – i.e., it is taken for granted *as if it were real*, just as I took my forbidden meal for granted until the occasion to question it arose.

Note that the clinical distinction between fantasy and reality does not depend on some absolute notion of objective "material" reality. The standard of what is real is provided by the patient, and it is not identical with her "psychic reality," i.e., with conscious or unconscious fantasy. Reality, and the related capacity to test reality, refers to the consistency of one's own experience as reliable and predictable. Every individual develops some capacity to use her judgment to consider whether an idea conforms to her experience.

If we take that as a rule for a personal definition of reality, the situations described heretofore as "psychic reality" are not real; rather, they are kept *unquestioned*, and if they were tested by the rule of congruence with experience, they would be judged *by the subject* to be unreal. (The motive for not testing is another fantasy that is not tested.) When the analyst calls into question the patient's allegiance to an unrealistic idea, she is making the judgment that *the patient's own* criteria of reality are being violated. The analyst may be mistaken, of course, but her expectation is that the patient will agree about the reality in question once her attention is drawn to it.

Reality and Perverse Defenses

The "split in the ego" to which Freud alluded refers to the bland tolerance of two contradictory positions: the perception of reality and the insistence on proceeding as if the perception did not count, *despite its having been perceived accurately*. This is sometimes described by making a distinction between "psychic" reality and "material" reality. As I have said, I believe it is incorrect to refer to a wishful *fantasy* as "reality" of any kind because, *when the patient chooses to do so*, she is fully capable of distinguishing fantasy from *her own view* of what is real. The definitive problem is not that the individual has a mistaken belief in her "psychic reality," nor is it that she is incapable of distinguishing fantasy from reality. The problem is in the license the patient takes to *keep her treasured beliefs untested*. The patient is troubled by the implications of facing *what she would recognize as real*, if she allowed the question to come up. So the patient casts doubt on the methodology that leads to the unwanted conclusions. She treats dreams as if they were real and perceptions as if they were dreams. If you catch her at it, the patient can acknowledge the unwanted facts – but will refuse to accept the consequences.

This attitude was expressed eloquently by the probation officer I mentioned in Chapter 4, who occasionally fondled the teenage girls in his charge. It was not that he did not know right from wrong, nor was he unaware of the potential consequences of his actions. But, as he himself put it, he "turned down the volume on reality" when it suited him to do so. In contrast to the neurotic compromise of altering, inhibiting, or disguising a wish that is perceived as dangerous, the perverse compromise is to disavow the significance of the reality – in this case, the perception of his own actions and their consequences. In other words, he chose to treat the unwanted perceptions as if they were not real *despite knowledge to the contrary*.

Another man, a lawyer, handled unwanted perceptions in a most lawyer-like fashion. When he did not want to face a troublesome fact, he would argue. His favorite expression was "One could make the case that." At those times he was careful *not* to consider whether the "case" was true or false in his estimation. At other times, I would point something out that he did not want to hear, and he would accept it "for the sake of argument" or he would "stipulate" to it. In other words, he would allow it on the condition that we took no action to determine the truth.

The defining characteristic of the perverse way of thinking is that potentially distressing perceptions, although noted, can be treated as if they did not matter. In Freud's example of fetishism, the disavowed reality is the perception of the female genital, and the motive for the disavowal is castration anxiety. But as Freud (1927) himself noted, the use of disavowal is not limited to the sexual perversions (p. 156). The issue of consequence is the turn of development that allows certain people to take such liberties with the testimony of their senses that they can set it aside when it threatens them. Such people apply the same self-deceiving tricks of mind to *any* disturbing reality.

Perverse defenses depend on a form of dishonesty, a disordered conscience that allows the subject to *act as if* she were unable to distinguish fantasy from reality. Sociopathy is its extreme manifestation. As analysts, we know that dishonesty is a human trait and it has its motivations. In his paper "Character perversion," Arlow (1971, pp. 177–94) writes about a "superego subverted by anxiety" or, we might add, by any intolerable affect. The superego's contribution to perception and reality testing (Weinshel, 1986) is compromised in the perverse view of reality.

Another Clinical Example

The following example may help illustrate the pervasive quality of the attitude toward reality I am trying to describe, as well as some of the problems it creates for analysis.

In complaining about his wife, a man in analysis described an interaction with her that had irritated him. She had noticed an ominous-looking mole on his arm and told him he should have it checked by a doctor. He was annoyed with her badgering. She should not have made him worry; she should be supportive and help him stop worrying (I heard this statement as a reference to me as well, but I chose not to address it for reasons I will mention later). He had not gone to the doctor.

After some discussion, it became apparent that he had noticed the mole as well. He had shrugged it off, telling himself that it had probably always been there, and his momentary worry had passed. He then proceeded to talk about what a hypochondriac he was. He wondered what it was in his past that made him so prone to bodily worries.

Although this was an important question, it was one we had already explored in some depth. The possibility of a masochistic need for suffering or punishment had been considered, among other meanings of his bodily worries. It did not seem to me then or now that this was a man who felt a need to suffer. There had been no hint of self-punitive or self-destructive trends. On the contrary, it had seemed in the past that he tended to blur the distinction between real and imagined ills in order to reassure himself that any bodily defect was illusory.

I was alerted from previous work to wonder aloud about his statement that the mole had "probably" always been there; had it, or hadn't it? When he let himself think about it, he realized he had noticed that the mole had changed in size and appearance recently; in fact, that was what had prompted his wife's remark. Now he was anxious again; he even had the "fantasy" that he had cancer. He was very troubled by how easily he got caught up in such fantasies and eager to investigate that propensity.

I commented that what was troubling him was not the fantasy but the reality of his changing mole, which he wanted desperately to discount by telling himself it was a fantasy. He seemed to recognize himself in this observation and was able to connect it with similar instances of disavowal that we had discussed. He wanted to pursue the psychological meaning of it as we had done in the past – for example, around certain confusions about whether something he had experienced had been a dream or a reality. He was able to see connections to certain ways his parents dealt with him as a child, telling him he had been dreaming when he had observed them engaged in activities they wanted to hide.

This line of thought was clearly germane and potentially very profitable to pursue, as it had been earlier in the analysis, but it was something of a rehash of previous work. It seemed to me that his line of enquiry represented yet another disavowal. I told him that I thought he was calming himself by making the terrifying physical reality of the mole into a "merely psychological" issue. Again, he recognized the defensive nature of the action and his motives for it, and, again, he tried to explore it as an "interesting hypothesis." Toward the end of the hour, I pointed out that there was much to understand about his ways of handling terrifying realities, but that no exploration of the meanings of his actions was going to make the mole less dangerous or reduce the need for him to see a doctor.

I have tried with this example both to demonstrate a series of disavowals of a terrifying reality and to give at least a hint of the stubborn persistence of the disavowing tendency in some patients that leads me to characterize it as an attitude toward reality.

At the end of the hour, I did not limit myself to the interpretation of the patient's disavowals; I also took a position on behalf of reality. As I said in the previous chapter, I believe that this is often a necessary component in the analysis of such patients; otherwise, the entire analytic enterprise can be turned to the service of the disavowing attitude by allowing the patient to construe her experience in analysis as "merely psychological," i.e., disconnected from her life problems.

I have suggested that it is misleading to speak of the patient's "psychic reality" in these cases, as if they subscribed to a different *kind* of reality from the consensual "material reality." Each of these patients was capable of judging what was real and what was not *by his own standards*, and each made efforts to avoid the consequences of that judgment. What is different is his attitude towards it and his unwillingness to draw compelling conclusions from it. He is not caught up in his unique "reality" any more than the rest of us; he is *evading* it in order to assert a *fantasy*. He is, by his own definition, unrealistic.

The Patient's Reality and the Analyst's Reality

Schwaber (1995) acknowledges that "there is no fact without theory" and that "we must utilize our own perspective … in order to locate that of another" (p. 559). But her clinical examples suggest that, *in principle*, with careful enough self-monitoring, it is not only possible but desirable to work exclusively with the patient's experience as if one were not influencing it. But in order to see oneself as entering into the patient's "psychic reality," one must also see oneself as able to suspend one's own. Schwaber's view is thus a paradox. What the analyst chooses to interpret, what the analyst is capable of noticing, what the analyst overlooks – all are unavoidable influences on the analytic material that are determined by the analyst's psychology. It is not possible to enter into the patient's experience without changing it. It is not possible to see things through the patient's eyes. Empathy is not the literal experiencing of what the patient experiences but the appreciation of what a situation would mean *to the analyst* if she were in similar circumstances.

Whereas Schwaber (1992) sees countertransference – in the sense of an interference in the work coming from the analyst – as due to a retreat from the patient's vantage point, I think there is equal danger in the analyst's temptation to overlook the fact that she is perceiving from the analyst's vantage point. The analyst's view of the patient's inner world belongs to the analyst, not to the patient.[1] As Renik (1993) has shown, the analyst's effort to set aside her own subjective view simply invites the patient to collude in ruling it off-limits for analytic consideration.

On the other hand, the analyst is in a position to be very authoritative about her own view of reality, once it is acknowledged as no more than that. And in work with patients who disavow their view of reality, it is imperative that the analyst be prepared to speak for the demands of reality – the patient's, where an internal contradiction is apparent, and the analyst's, in any case – in order to address the ways they are disavowed. It is not only impossible to "enter into" the patient's psychic reality, it is also counterproductive to try to do so, especially in work with those patients whose consciences allow them to shrug off the consequences of their own judgment of reality.

Whereas the concept of psychic reality corrected an imbalance in our thinking by giving fantasy its due, work with patients with perverse defenses depends on giving reality its due. Here we can see a potential for misuse of the concept of "psychic reality": If the analyst tries to be so respectful of the patient's fantasy life as to treat it as a "reality," she cannot identify the patient's evasions, falsifications, or deceits. The analyst will tacitly collude with the patient's clinging to the attitude that painful reality can be treated as if it were just an illusion. Then the analysis itself becomes an "as-if" affair, losing its rootedness in the patient's real life; the analysis itself becomes a fetish object (Renik, 1992), protecting the patient from the perceived dangers of reality.

As noted in the previous chapter, work with such patients is exceptionally difficult precisely because treatment realities are subject to the same disregard as other painful realities. It requires diligence and persistence in calling attention to the various forms of disavowal as they are brought into play. This means that the analyst must be active in ascertaining what the patient sees as the real state of affairs, and what reality the two parties can agree upon. The perverse attitude amounts to an evasion of responsibility for one's own reality. The analyst's failure to call a spade a spade and identify that evasion, out of a well-meaning attempt to be respectful of the patient's alternative "psychic reality," is an abrogation of the analyst's responsibility to help the patient face the world as she knows it to be.

Note

1   For a compelling discussion of this position, see Wilson (2020, pp. 49–74).

References

Arlow, J.A. (1971). *Psychoanalysis: Clinical theory and practice*. International Universities Press.

Arlow, J.A. (1985). The concept of psychic reality and related problems. *Journal of the American Psychoanalytic Association, 33*(3), 521–35.

Freud, S. (1900). *The interpretation of dreams*. SE *4–5*.

Freud, S. (1927). Fetishism. SE *21*, 149–58.

Levenson, E.A. (1988). Real frogs in imaginary gardens. Facts and fantasies in psychoanalysis. *Psychoanalytic Inquiry, 8*(4), 552–67.

Loewald, H.W. (1952). The problem of defense and the neurotic interpretation of reality. *The International Journal of Psychoanalysis, 33*, 444–9.

Renik, O. (1992). Use of the analyst as a fetish. *The Psychoanalytic Quarterly, 61*(4), 542–63.

Renik, O. (1993). Analytic interaction: Conceptualizing technique in light of the analyst's irreducible subjectivity. *The Psychoanalytic Quarterly, 62*(4), 553–71.

Schwaber, E.A. (1992). Countertransference: The analyst's retreat from the patient's vantage point. *The International Journal of Psychoanalysis, 73*(2), 349–61.

Schwaber, E.A. (1995). Towards a definition of the term and concept of interaction. *The International Journal of Psychoanalysis, 76*(3), 557–64.

Weinshel, E.M. (1986). Perceptual distortions during analysis: Some observations on the role of the superego in reality testing. In A.D. Richards & M.S. Willick (Eds.), *Psychoanalysis. The science of mental conflict. Essays in honor of Charles Brenner* (pp. 353–374). Analytic Press.

Wilson, M. (2020). *The analyst's desire. The ethical foundation of clinical practice.* Bloomsbury Academic.

Chapter 6

The Object-Preserving Function of Sadomasochism

Clinical practice has not taken sufficient account of the distinction between what belongs to conjoining and what belongs to destroying in sadomasochistic relations. This is partly a consequence of a plethora of uses of the terms sadism and masochism. They have been used to name perverse sexual practices, acts of cruelty, acts of aggression, acts of destruction, "component instincts" of libido, aspects of normal psychosexual development, character traits, manifestations of the death instinct, and a turning of one against the other. In what follows I would like to review how this multiplicity of uses arose and to advocate attention to the implication that sadism, masochism, and sadomasochism contain an object-preserving component. My hope is that this will make it easier for us to be sure we are speaking the same language, no matter what our theoretical dialect. I will argue that sadism and masochism are best understood as two expressions of the same tendency, and that the function of sadomasochism is to control an object in order to maintain a connection.

The aim common to most uses of the term sadism is to control another person. Grotstein (1998), for example, sees no need to elaborate when he makes the distinction between "destructiveness (hate) and sadism (control)" (p. 88). On the other hand, even a superficial glance at the literature reveals the prevalence of the conflation of the two ideas. For example, Blos (1991) uses the phrase "destructive sadistic rage" (p. 424) in a case report. Giovacchini (1990) refers to "sadistic destructive impulses" (p. 13). Casoni (2002) refers to "sadistic destructiveness" (p. 157). In contrast, the summary of a panel report on sadism and masochism (Cooper & Sacks, 1991) reported Cooper's views as follows:

> The issue of sadism is still very much unresolved in Cooper's view ....
> Sadism carries the traditional connotation of a drive derived from sexuality. This differs from aggression, which arises from different sources and without the implication that it is gratifying in and of itself in some broadened sexual way. The relation between sadism and masochism remains obscure.
>
> (Cooper & Sacks, 1991, p. 225)

DOI: 10.4324/9781003360391-8

Gabbard (2000) wrote about hatred, saying, "To hate is to *hold onto an object* in an unforgiving way" (p. 411; italics added). He elaborated, "hatred binds the patient to the hated object … While rage tries to remove the object, hatred forges an unbreakable bond between object and self" (Gabbard, 2000, p. 412). These are all important contributions, but even in this short sampling we see the equation of hate and control (Gabbard), the opposition of aggression and control (Grotstein, Cooper), the opposition of hate and rage (Gabbard), and the equation of sadism and destructiveness (Blos, Giovacchini, Casoni).

Of course, we must always distinguish between sadism as an inferred unconscious motive and sadism as a manifest behavior.[1] I assume that all manifest behaviors obey the principle of multiple function (Waelder, 2007). I propose that it is clinically crucial to try to tease out the various aims, including the sadistic/controlling, the hateful, and the aggressive, rather than to lump them all together under the term sadism. My goal is to help us attend to what Gabbard called the binding function in sadomasochism. I suggest that we pay more attention to the effort to *maintain an object tie by controlling the object*, in contradistinction to other aims, especially aggressive ones. In what follows I will try to show how the clarification I am advocating matters in clinical work. In addition, I will take a brief look at the fluidity that seems to exist between sadistic and masochistic roles in human behavior and consider a possible developmental explanation. I will end with an observation about the role of sadomasochism so understood, in adult sexual perverse practices. But to begin, I would like to follow how Freud's thinking about sadism and masochism developed as his theory of instincts changed. Freud's odyssey from one theory to the next, his inconsistent application of his own ideas, and especially his problematic view of primary masochism have left us a legacy of confusion about the vital issues arising from sadism and masochism.

The Evolution of Freud's Views on Sadomasochism

The *Standard Edition* translation of the *Three Essays on the Theory of Sexuality* (Freud, 1905) provides a convenient condensation of the changes in Freud's thinking over time. Freud revised the work three times, the last in 1924. As a result, the work is a palimpsest revealing Freud's thinking in four different periods. In the original version, Freud provided Krafft-Ebing's definition of sadistic and masochistic *perversion* (that is, behavior) as the active and passive forms of pleasure in humiliation or subjection (Freud, 1905, p. 157). It is of note that, at that time, Freud used the word "aggressiveness" to describe a male's desire to subjugate in sexuality (Freud, 1905, p. 157). He concluded with an inference of what lay behind the behavior: "Thus sadism would correspond to an *aggressive* component of the sexual instinct which has become independent and exaggerated" (Freud, 1905, p. 158; italics added). At this stage of Freud's thinking, aggression would have been included among the (non-libidinal) self-preservative instincts, but it was not accorded anything like equal stature with libido; his usage often seems more along the lines of ordinary language than technical terminology.

Freud was emphatic about the relation between sadistic and masochistic *behavior* in 1905: "The most remarkable feature of this perversion is that its active and passive forms are habitually found to occur together in the same individual .... *A sadist is always at the same time a masochist*" (p. 159; italics added). This is a key observation that seems to disappear in future writings. In the 1915 revision, he wrote "It may be doubted at first whether [masochism] can ever occur as a primary phenomenon or whether, on the contrary, it may not invariably arise from a transformation of sadism" (Freud, 1905, p. 158). A footnote Freud added in 1924 tells us that he had subsequently changed his opinion in favor of the existence of a primary erotogenic masochism (Freud, 1905, p. 158, footnote 2). I will consider this change later on.

In the 1915 revision of the second of the *Three Essays*, Freud introduced what came to be known as the psychosexual stages of development. In his description of the "sadistic-anal" phase of development, he wrote:

> Here the opposition between the two currents, which runs through all sexual life, is already developed; they cannot yet, however, be described as "masculine" and "feminine," but only as "active" and "passive." The *activity* is put into operation by the instinct for mastery.
> (Freud, 1905, p. 198; italics in original)

A Digression: The Instinct for Mastery

The instinct for mastery is, to me, another concept whose ambiguity is hidden in its developmental history. It is used variously to describe mastery of one's own body, for example muscular and sphincter control in the anal phase; mastery of others in the (also ambiguous) sense of sadism and masochism; and mastery of the helplessness of traumatic overstimulation in the form of turning passive into active. The sadistic-anal phase, as Freud described it, is an object-related phase: "Both of these currents [i.e., active and passive] have objects ... In this phase, therefore, sexual polarity and an *extraneous* object are already observable" (Freud, 1905, p. 198–9; italics added).

Thus the mastery in this context is of an external object. So it seems that, at this point in Freud's thinking (*ca.* 1915, as it were, between dual instinct theories), mastery – as an aspect of sadism – was understood as a libidinal instinct subject to gratification in an interaction with an object. In his discussion of the "fort-da" game (which I will discuss further in what follows), Freud seems to wrestle with the placement of mastery in instinct theory – in the very publication where he first articulates the death instinct (Freud, 1920).

But in a very late summary of his ultimate dual instinct theory, Freud (1933a) gives these two examples of the "alloying" of the erotic and destructive instincts:

Thus, for instance, the instinct of self-preservation is certainly of an erotic kind, but it must nevertheless have aggressiveness at its disposal if it is to fulfill its purpose. *So, too, the instinct of love* [N.B.: not "libido"], *when it is directed towards an object, stands in need of some contribution from the instinct for mastery* if it is in any way to obtain possession of that object.

(pp. 209–10; italics added)

It would seem that Freud ultimately settled on identifying mastery as a derivative of the destructive instinct, to be alloyed with libido in object-love.

Aggression, Sadism, and Masochism

With the formulation of the death instinct in *Beyond the Pleasure Principle* (1920) Freud altered the status of aggression. At this point he conceived of it as the projection of a biologically determined self-destructive trend, a kind of psychological entropy that opposed the life-instinct (Eros) that manifested itself as libido. He used the concept to explain various apparently self-attacking actions that seemed to run counter to the pleasure principle – among them masochism.

The notion of a "primary masochism" that does not originate in sadistic urges, tentatively proposed earlier (1920), was taken as a fact in *The Economic Problem of Masochism* (1924). From this point on, at least one form of masochistic behavior was explained as a derivative of the death instinct, and thus independent of libido. In subsequent work Freud refers to "the *destructive* cathexes belonging to the sadistic phase" (1926, p. 114; italics added).

In his last word on the subject, in a summary of the psychosexual stages of development, Freud (1940) wrote:

> During [the] oral phase sadistic impulses already occur sporadically along with the appearance of the teeth. Their extent is far greater in the second phase, which we describe as the sadistic-anal one, because satisfaction is then sought in aggression and in the excretory function. Our justification for including aggressive urges under the libido is based on the view that sadism is an instinctual fusion of purely libidinal and purely destructive urges, a fusion which thenceforward persists uninterruptedly.
>
> (Freud, 1940, p. 154)

In a footnote to that passage, he added:

> The question arises whether the satisfaction of purely destructive instinctual impulses can be felt as pleasure, whether pure destructiveness without any libidinal admixture occurs. Satisfaction of the death instinct remaining in the ego seems not to produce feelings of pleasure, though masochism represents a fusion that is entirely analogous to sadism.
>
> (Freud, 1940, p.154, footnote)

In these two statements, Freud has shifted from a description of underlying instinctual derivatives (e.g., primary masochism) to a discussion of manifest *behavior* as a fusion of instincts. I believe this double use of the same words has contributed to the conceptual ambiguity that persists today.

For my thesis, the importance of Freud's reformulation of instinct theory has to do with the elevation of the role of aggression as on a par with, and with the opposite aim of, libido. It does not matter, for my present purposes, whether one conceives of an externalization of the death instinct or of a primary aggressive drive. Once aggression is granted a major role, Freud reconceptualizes various clinical presentations in terms of the fusion (or regressive de-fusion) of aggression and libido. Freud's mature formulation of sadism and masochism incorporates these ideas as follows:

> Our hypothesis is that there are two essentially different classes of instincts: the sexual instincts, understood in the widest sense – Eros, if you prefer that name – and the aggressive instincts, whose aim is destruction .... [I]n sadism and in masochism we have before us two excellent examples of a mixture of the two classes of instinct .... [W]e are led to the view that masochism is older than sadism, and that sadism is the destructive instinct directed outwards, thus acquiring the characteristic of aggressiveness.
>
> (Freud, 1933b, p. 103–5)

Here I think Freud continues to blur the distinction between sadism and masochism as "component instincts" (1905) and as manifest actions. Furthermore, he has concluded (unfortunately, in my view) that both are consequences of the destructive instinct.

In thus reconceiving sadism and masochism, Freud seems also to have abandoned the clinical observation he made in 1905 that sadism and masochism seem invariably to be paired within the same individual. His view of sadism and masochism as active and passive forms of the same instinct seems also to be mitigated by seeing one (masochism) as "older" than the other.

Freud's most often cited reason for writing *Beyond the Pleasure Principle* was that he had observed (in sexual masochism, in the compulsion to repeat, and in other phenomena) actions that seemed to be motivated by something beyond or "more primitive than [the pleasure principle] and independent of it" (Freud, 1920, p. 17). But it is worth recalling that he also had to deal with the inadequacy of the pleasure principle as formulated (decreased excitation, or some complex ratio or rate of increasing and decreasing excitation) to describe what is ultimately pleasurable (Freud, 1920, pp. 7–10). What remains of the tension reduction principle is subsumed under the death instinct (the "Nirvana principle"; Freud, 1920, p. 56). In his final reformulation, Freud (1940) wrote:

> After long hesitations and vacillations we have decided to assume the existence of only two basic instincts, *Eros* and *the destructive instinct* .... The aim of the first of these basic instincts is to establish ever greater unities and to preserve them thus – in short, to bind together; the aim of the second is, on the contrary, to undo connections and so to destroy things. In the case of the destructive instinct we may suppose that its final aim is to lead what is living into an inorganic state. For this reason we also call it the *death instinct*.
>
> (p. 148; italics in original)

Freud's formulation of Eros addresses the issue of what drives growth and change. In the original tension-reduction model of the pleasure principle, it is hard to see why life exists at all and even harder to see how change is possible. The old model seems to imply that everything strives for death (zero tension) and dissolution (maximum entropy). With the reformulation of Eros, Freud introduces a life force that counters the forces of inertia and entropy. It gives a name for the tendency in organisms to grow in the direction of more complex organization, heretofore ignored in the theory. It is in this reconception of libido as the psychological expression of Eros that human development and change find motivation (Loewald, 1966, Chapter 5, pp. 62–3). Unfortunately, Freud did not apply his formulation of Eros to include sadomasochism itself.

The Developmental Assumptions of the Present Chapter

Up to this point I have been using Freud's language: pre- and post-structural, pre- and post-death instinct. I have focused exclusively on the "instinctual" and largely ignored the rest of childhood development because that is the way Freud first recognized the universality of sadism in young children. But now, as I begin to elaborate my own hypotheses, I would like to spell out the minimal developmental assumptions on which my subsequent ideas are based.

I assume that, at some point in the course of self/object differentiation, pleasure (or the avoidance of pain) and aggression become motivating forces in the world of others. From that point on, one of the ways to distinguish object-directed aims is on the basis of whether, in Freud's words, the aim is to bind together or to break apart. Whatever names we attach to these classes of aims (for Freud – Eros and the death instinct), they work in opposite directions.

For the purposes of this paper it does not matter if *aggression* is understood as a manifestation of the death instinct (Freud after 1920, the Kleinians), or if it is seen as reactive to early frustration (the British independent group, the relational approaches) or to narcissistic injury (self psychology); nor does it matter if the "drives" are biological givens (Freud), or if they are organized out of an earlier undifferentiated state along with self-object differentiation (Loewald). Nor does it matter for our present purposes if we see object-seeking as a derivative of bodily pleasure, as Freud did, or as a fundamental tendency, for example as Fairbairn (1963) did. By no means am I saying that these distinctions are unimportant; I am saying that they are beside the point of this discussion.

I accept Freud's observation that, at some point in early childhood development within what he called the sadistic-anal phase, sadism appears naturally as one such derivative of pleasure aimed at an object. By way of contrast, note that the "ruthlessness" described by Winnicott (1965, pp. 22–3) in the younger infant does not take account of the external object.

I assume that the capacity for full object relations, i.e., the appreciation of another as an independent self, develops gradually from an earlier state in which others exist only as means to, or obstacles to, a subject-centered end. Again, for my immediate purposes it does not matter if this is understood as preceded by a primary undifferentiated state, an "all id" autoerotic state, a (part-)object-seeking state, or a "core self" (Stern, 1985, p. 69) present in the earliest months of life.

I am being as spare as I can in describing these assumptions. My hope is that some analysts will recognize these ideas as compatible with their own and those analysts who do not share these assumptions will be clear on where we differ.

Fort-Da Revisited

At this point, I would like to revisit one of Freud's observations. Along with the formulation of the death instinct, *Beyond the Pleasure Principle* included an observation of a game played by a boy of one and a half. The boy had a spool attached to a piece of string. He would throw the spool over the edge of his cot, saying "fort" ("gone") as he did so. Then he would pull it back by the string with a joyful "da" ("there"). Freud connected the game to the mother's temporary absence (1920, p. 15). Since the mother's departure was clearly not pleasurable, Freud raised the question of how this game could be motivated by the pleasure principle, but by the end of his discussion Freud has made the case that the game is indeed so motivated:

> [When his mother left, the child] was in a *passive* situation – he was overpowered by the experience; but, by repeating it, unpleasurable though it was, as a game, he took on an *active* part. These efforts might be put down to an instinct for mastery that was acting independently of whether the memory was in itself pleasurable or not. But still another interpretation may be attempted. Throwing away the object so that it was "gone" might satisfy an impulse of the child's, which was suppressed in his actual life, to revenge himself on his mother for going away from

him. In that case it would have a defiant meaning: "All right, then, go away! I don't need you. I'm sending you away myself."[2] ... We are therefore left in doubt as to whether the impulse to work over in the mind some overpowering experience so as to make oneself master of it can find expression as a primary event, and independently of the pleasure principle.

(Freud, 1920, p. 16)

Here Freud finds that "mastery," in the form of turning passively endured experience into actively created experience, may be a pleasurable gratification of a vengeful wish.

I would like to offer an additional interpretation of the nature of the pleasure in the "fort-da" game: I would like to call attention to the function of the string. It makes sense to me that the child takes a vengeful pleasure in his activity, and that there may also be a satisfaction of an aggressive, destructive urge toward the mother. But what strikes me as an important neglected element is the representation of the mother as under the control of the child – the spool is tied to him. Many will recognize the similarity to Winnicott's (1953) transitional object – "the first 'not-me' possession" (p. 89). If the string represents the tie to the mother, then the child's connection to the mother is preserved and enjoyed on his terms. Then the child's (adultified) message, besides being vengeful and defiant, might be "I am not at the mercy of your whims. In fact, I am the one who determines when you come and go. I can dictate your presence on my schedule."

Aggression and Sadism: A Proposal

What I have just described, I think, is a clinically useful way to think about sadism, as distinct from aggression. As Freud pointed out, the two aims typically occur in varying admixtures in a given situation (i.e., in manifest behavior), but it is often important to distinguish what is sadistic (in service of maintaining an object tie) from what is aggressive (in service of destroying one) in a clinical moment, so that one may consider the opposing contributions of each. Furthermore, theoretically conflating sadism and aggression may lead to problematic and erroneous conclusions – if, for example, a patient's effort to control the analyst and the analytic situation, in order to preserve them, is interpreted *only* as his envy-driven wish to destroy the analysis or the analyst.

From this perspective, outwardly directed "mastery" seems intimately related to sadism as connectedness. The maintenance of a master–slave relationship (or some derivative of it) is precisely the kind of tie to an object that is defined as sadism. A master, in order to be a master, must control a slave. In order to do so, he must preserve the relationship. A master who kills his slave, or a torturer who kills his subject, has failed; he has lost his relationship and his role.

Sadomasochism and Reversibility: A Developmental Speculation

I would like to return to two of Freud's observations of sadism and masochism already cited from the *Three Essays*. First, that the two trends occur together in the same individual: "A sadist is always at the same time a masochist" (1905, p. 159). Second, concomitant with the development of sadism, a polarity between activity and passivity is established and the role of an "extraneous object" of the subject's sadism and masochism is in play (Freud, 1905, pp. 198–9; passage added in 1915). We may be able to understand these observations and draw some further tentative conclusions if we briefly consider the course of development of relations to that "extraneous object."

If we think of a developmental line of self and object definition as emerging from an initial undifferentiated state[3] and ultimately arriving at a state in which other people are appreciated as fully autonomous beings who exist even when absent, we imply a transitional state. As the mother and infant begin to emerge as separate, I would speculate that the mother is at first experienced as a "me-possession" – that is to say, as something intermediate between the child *being* (at one with, identified with) her and *having* her, perhaps as if she were a part of his body that he could look at.

As the mother moves further toward separateness she becomes more of a "not-me" *possession* (Winnicott, 1953; italics added), as if she were under the control of the child, as in the "fort-da" game. The gradualness or piecemeal process of self-object differentiation suggests an intermediate, unstable equilibrium, and possibly an oscillation, between identification (being) and object relating (having). Such a state would be marked by efforts to individuate, accompanied by fears of losing the object, and feeling the need to merge with the mother, accompanied by threats of losing the emerging self (Loewald, 1951, p. 16).

These observations suggest a possible explanation of the phenomenon of the pairing of sadism and masochism in the service of object relations that Freud observed in 1905. The state of ego development (especially the object-relating functions) in the beginnings of separation and individuation creates the conditions not only for the well-known power struggles but also for psychic role reversibility. The child begins to recognize objects, but the realization of their independence is threatening prior to the establishment of object constancy (Mahler et al., 1975) because he is not yet equipped to trust what he cannot control. Thus, relations at this stage are marked by efforts to control the object as a possession and by the perception of the object as attempting to control the self. But the differentiation of self and object is still fluid; once that is consolidated, the task of controlling the object is replaced by the challenge of relating to it in its independence. Until then, that fluidity allows the child to move psychically between the roles of controller and controlled, i.e., to imagine and live out a kind of relating, for which the script is the same – sadomasochism – regardless of the role being played at a given moment.

Loewald (1973) proposed that internalizing processes are the basis of psychic structure formation, including self and object differentiation (p. 12). This view suggests that the movement between sadistic and masochistic roles originates in the alternation of projection and introjection during this period of development. Introjection and projection tentatively (and reversibly) assign previously undifferentiated states as belonging to oneself (being) or to one's object (having).

The key to the above situation is that I am describing sadomasochistic relating, in the sense of controlling–being controlled, as a developmentally appropriate mode of relating for the child on the way to full object relations. Freud (1905) suggested that being told by a parent to control one's sphincters may be the first instance of an individual's having to renounce an instinct for social reasons (p. 187, footnote). At first this can make no sense to the child except as a submission to the whims of a loved object (Anthony, 1957, p. 148). The child may then comply out of love or refuse in defiance; in either case, the child's working definition of love – the judgment about what happens between two people that keeps them together – will be a dyad of dominance and submission. In this context we might consider that the arbitrary "no" characteristic of toddlers (often in an imitation of the parent's voice) represents an internalized version of a parental prerogative – in other words, part of an alternation between seeing oneself as the parent and as the child. Thus, the awareness of generational differences at this stage may be mapped onto the reversible distinction between activity and passivity, just as Freud suggested was the case for sexual differences.

Spitz (1958) describes the origin of the "period of stubbornness" (p. 378) as a consequence of handling a conflict between the infant (age 15 months in his study) and a frustrating parent, which is internalized via an "identification with the *aggressor*" (p. 383; italics added). But he also notes that the identification is motivated by the libidinal attachment to the parent. It might be more accurate to propose an "identification with the controller" that leaves room for the child's interpretation of the parent's frustrating (controlling) actions as (sadistic) signs of love.[4]

What Does This Distinction Look Like?

We expect that, in the course of normal development, the child will come to feel relatively safe with the independence of the object, although, as we know, this is far from always the case. As an extreme illustration I might mention a profoundly isolated psychotic woman with whom I worked for over twenty years (presented in Chapter 7). As our time together progressed, she became more and more controlling of me and what I was allowed to say, until I was restricted to five words: yes, no, I don't know. If I departed even in small ways from that script, she would feel "raped."

I mention this example to illustrate an extreme of what sadomasochistic relating might look like. I am not making a point about treatment. There were, no doubt, multiple functions to the interaction, some of which may be obvious, some not. I do not even presume to compare the relative weights of the various possible functions. The inference I do want to draw from the above is based on one feature of the case – namely, that it went on for *twenty years*, during much of which we both felt tortured and we both felt like torturers. The sadism of her rigid, controlling script for the interaction, the masochism of her experience of being tortured and raped, and the fluidity of the roles of controller/controlled effectively *bound us together*.

In this instance, I had no shortage of murderous feelings toward the patient, along with other reactions. I think most of us would entertain the idea that those feelings signaled something about the patient, as well as about me. But if one assumes that my murderous feeling is a simple transcription of the patient's experience, one might be prone to overlook what I am now calling the sadomasochistic component to the interaction – namely, the patient's effort to maintain the attachment to me by controlling me. In this instance it was also true that the murderous wishes were my own; I even found them comforting. In any case, I found it useful to separate the patient's (and my) aggression, conceived as a wish to rupture the relationship, from what I am calling the sadistic aim: to maintain the connection by controlling it. I believe they were both present but worked in opposite directions.

A Less Extreme Clinical Example

The case I have just described is not the kind of problem one typically confronts in an analytic practice. A commoner problem is illustrated in my work with Geraldo, a lawyer who came to see me because of problems in his marriage, tension at work, and difficulty making decisions. Geraldo described how his wife nagged him constantly about a "promise" he had made her when they were married that after he got established at his firm he would transfer to their east coast office, which would be nearer to her family. The quotes around "promise" are to indicate his qualification: "Yes, I said it, but it wasn't really a promise."

At the time we began, he was in a position to transfer but could not make up his mind. It did not seem like a bad idea; he saw pros and cons; he just hadn't decided. The tension became apparent when his wife started pressing the issue: The more she wanted to go, the more he felt unable to decide. He blamed the pressure she put on him for his paralysis and implied that, if she would just let up, he would be able to make a choice.

It was a predictable irony that, as an initial consultation extended into an ongoing treatment and then into an analysis, the analysis became a major factor in the conflict between Geraldo and his wife. At the beginning I tried to show him that, by starting analysis, he was making a decision to stay in town. He seemed to understand that but quickly turned it into a situation in which, since the analysis was undertaken to help him make a decision, once he made a decision he would leave. As one might imagine, the analysis itself then took on a one foot in, one foot out quality. He soon began to see me as having an overridingly selfish interest in his decision, although the form of the selfishness he assigned me oscillated between my wanting to force him to stay and my wanting to kick him out.

As time went on, Geraldo made it clear that he did not find me at all helpful. When I said something, he would typically respond in one of two ways: Either he would parse my words microscopically to find the flaw in them, or he would say "I don't disagree," which conveyed the notion that what I said was too obvious to address – and, incidentally, was somehow different from agreeing with me. At times his view of me, ranging from being useless to causing him pain, would be phrased as a threat to ruin my reputation – followed by the words, "No, I'm kidding!" I was not laughing.

After the analysis had gone on for some time, it became clear that Geraldo's state of being "on the verge" of a decision, e.g., giving up his unhelpful analyst and moving to the east coast, was not temporary or transitional; in fact, he lived "on the verge," uncommitted, tormenting his wife and analyst as he felt tormented by us.

At one point early in the analysis I made the observation that he almost invariably arrived five minutes after the start of our time. He referred to it as a typical problem of his, of being late; he gets caught up in whatever he is doing and does not want to interrupt himself to leave for an appointment. I commented that calling it being "late" did not seem quite right. After all, he always arrived at exactly the same time; in that sense he was in fact very punctual. He realized that he did not like to spend time in the waiting room; he didn't even like the phrase "waiting room": "I don't like to wait on people." I noted the phrase "wait *on*" rather than "wait *for*" and asked about it. He thought of waiters "servicing" people. "Servicing," I said; "different from serving?" He got uncomfortable, acknowledged he had an "icky" thought, but then got caught up in criticizing my tone of voice, which he felt was accusing him of something.

It was some time later – in his own time – that Geraldo got around to acknowledging the "icky" homosexual act he had pictured. It is important to note that I heard something in my tone of voice at the same time he did. I thought I sounded a little like a lawyer conducting a cross-examination. It seemed that we were enacting the adversarial approach to a relationship that I was trying to address. He then wanted to argue whether the "icky" thought was actually his or an artifact of the analysis; that is, he wanted to insist that it was me forcing something into him.

Once I heard my own controlling tone, I caught on to the longing for me that was expressed in disguised fashion in our debates – or, as we later came to think of them, our wrestling matches. I came to think of this sort of inter-action as the kind of intimacy with which he was most comfortable.

I hope this description is adequate to suggest how, in both his marriage and in his analytic relationship, Geraldo enacted (and drew us into enactments of) scenarios about being controlled that he used to control the other. In his mind, the only safe way to love people was to bind them to him, to control them in order to be assured of being loved back. The sadomasochistic com-ponent was plain, and there was no doubt that aggression also played a role in Geraldo's actions. Yet I think it would have been a mistake in this case to think of aggression as the only motivating force – that is, to focus on the destructive aims of his behavior. In my view, his sadomasochism was a des-perate effort to preserve something that he imagined to be fragile.[5]

As I put it together, Geraldo's sadism served to reassure him that he could control both himself and his love object. It helped him maintain what he felt was an optimal distance from me – not too close, but never unavailable. Once I noticed my own participation in the power struggle, I was able to see that he was more at home with his aggression – that is, it was more consciously available and therefore subject to his will – than he was with his affectionate and/or sexual longings. When at a later date we did take up his aggression, it was his use of it as a counter to the "icky" feelings that was more prominent.

I offer this very ordinary example to illustrate my thinking, not to attempt to prove anything. I think it is useful to distinguish the sadomasochistic from the aggressive contribution to manifest behavior, and also to notice how one may be used to counteract the other. If we conflate the libidinal (object-preserving) and the aggressive (object-destroying) components under the heading of sadism, it is easier to miss one or the other.

Sadomasochism and Perversion

I would like to turn briefly to a consideration of how the differentiation between sadomasochism and aggression may add something to our understanding of sexual perversion. I wish to make two things clear at the outset. First, I want to avoid an almost inevitable confusion. I am not talking about sadomaso-chism as a perverse practice, but rather the extent to which sadomasochism is common to all forms of sexual perversion. The discussion would apply equally to, say, fetishism or obligatory transvestism. Second, I have no intention of reviewing the extensive and ever-growing literature on the subject of perver-sion; nor do I imply any social judgment about elective sexual practices. What I am talking about are sexual practices experienced as compulsory.

If we are to retain the term sexual perversion at all, the one indispensable part of its definition should be its compulsive, ritualistic nature. The sex lives of some people are organized around a specific, obligatory, predetermined script, an assignment of roles from which neither party can depart. In order for this to be the case, the subject has to control his[6] partner, or at least to convince himself that he is controlling his partner. In other words, sado-masochism as I am using the term is an element common to all perverse sexuality.

It follows that sexual perversion is another subject for which understanding depends on how one conceives of the contributions of the erotic and the aggressive in sadomasochism. For example, Stoller (1974) wrote, "the term 'perversion' implies consciously preferred, habitual sexual fantasy or acts at whose root lies hostility." The acts themselves are not pathognomonic; rather, "perversion lies in the meaning of the act, wherein is hatred and a need to damage, not love, one's partner .... The study of perversion is the study of hostility more than libido" (Stoller, 1974, pp. 428–9). He concludes his article by advocating more analytic study of perversions "for clues [to] how aggression (activity) is converted into hostility (hatred and violence)" (Stoller, 1974, p. 433).

My impression is that Stoller is mixing his instinctual metaphors. Hostility and hatred, in Stoller's formulation, are derivatives of aggression – that is, they are expressions of the wish to destroy. But if instead we entertain the possibility that perverse practices are grounded in the sadomasochistic need to *control* the object, then we are in a position to consider a perversion as an act of love as understood by the actor – controlling love or damaging love, dicta-torial love or punishing love – but a love in which the partner is constrained from opting out.

In the clinical situation it is typically the case that the perversion will be enacted in the transference. If, as Stoller suggests, hatred is prominent, and if it is a derivative of aggression, then one would expect that the patient will attack the analyst in some form or other. I have not confirmed that in my work, except in the form of the patient's attempts to dictate the terms of engagement. Of course, every case is different, but, in general, I have not found that focusing on the presumed attack has been especially helpful. But when I have been able to see the object-preserving aim in the patient's actions, in and out of the transference, I have found the anxiety underlying it to be more accessible. I hope other analysts might compare their own experiences and see if they come to similar conclusions.

Summary and Concluding Remarks

As we have seen, Freud's thinking about sadism and masochism changed over time, largely but not entirely in parallel with the evolution of his instinct theory. The situation has been further complicated by Freud's somewhat inconsistent use of some key ideas, notably aggression and mastery. My impression has been that clinical practice has not taken sufficient account of the distinction between what belongs to conjoining and what belongs to destroying in sadomasochistic relations. I have tried to show that a clarifica-tion of that distinction, and in particular the recognition of the effort to bind oneself to an object via sadomasochistic control, as opposed to the effort to destroy an object via aggression, is often clinically important.

I have argued that recognizing the inherently dual nature of sadism and masochism – the reversibility of roles – expands our understanding of the clinical situation, including the transference. I have speculated that the fluidity of roles may be a persistence or regressive reemergence of the uncompleted developmental task of moving from identification to object-relation. Role reversibility may represent the oscillation between being (identifying with) one's object and having it.

I have offered the suggestion that sadomasochism, as a mode of relating appropriate to the developmental challenges faced in toddlerhood, is an element common to all sexual perversion and explains the rigidity of action (the "script") in perverse practices. It is a way to deny the threatening experience of dealing with a desired object who is independent of the subject's will.

I have had the impression that the object-preserving meaning of sadomasochistic relating has been relatively neglected lately in favor of emphasizing its destructive aims. Nonetheless, it has not been my intention to argue that one should always take up sadomasochistic *behavior* in terms of its inferred erotic meaning *instead of*, or even *before*, taking up aggressive derivatives. That is a clinical decision that can only be made in context. My central point is that, if one does not consider the libidinal meaning of sadism and its components separately from aggression, one risks missing powerful motives shaping the patient's life. People treat other people with love, hate, fear, and indifference; as analysts we cannot afford to ignore any of those trends.

Notes

1 I think we should also distinguish hate as an affect from our inferences about sadism and masochism, but I will not pursue that point here.

2 This interpretation is consistent with Cooper's (1988) formulation of the function of masochism as protecting the infant from the narcissistic blow of facing his helplessness.

3 I find Loewald's (1951) developmental ideas compelling, but the only developmental assumption I think would be incompatible with the speculation I am advancing is one that presumes self and object constancy to be present from birth. Even Stern's (1985) observations include the notion of an alteration of the sense of the relation between self and reality that unfolds over time.

4 For examples of later pathological consequences of a child's interpreting parental sadism as love, see Berliner (1958) and Renik (1991).

5 It is beyond the scope of this report to explore why he thought relationships, ours included, were fragile. Suffice it to say he was convinced since childhood that he was unlovable.

6 I choose the male pronoun here because the best understood sexual perversions seem to be far more prevalent among men than among women, but the argument I am advancing does not require a gender distinction.

References

Anthony, E.J. (1957). An experimental approach to the psychopathology of childhood: Encopresis. *British Journal of Medical Psychology, 30*, 146–75.

Berliner, B. (1958). The role of object relations in moral masochism. *The Psychoanalytic Quarterly, 27*, 38–56.

Blos, P., Jr. (1991). Sadomasochism and the defense against recall of painful affect. *Journal of the American Psychoanalytic Association, 39*(2), 417–30.

Casoni, D. (2002). "Never Twice Without Thrice:" An outline for the understanding of traumatic neurosis. *The International Journal of Psychoanalysis, 83*(1), 137–59.

Cooper, A.M. (1988). The narcissistic-masochistic character. In R.A. Glick & D.I. Meyers (Eds.), *Masochism. Current psychoanalytic perspectives* (pp. 117–38). The Analytic Press.

Cooper, A.M., & Sacks, M.H. (1991). Sadism and masochism in character disorder and resistance. *Journal of the American Psychoanalytic Association, 39*, 215–26.

Fairbairn, W.D. (1963). Synopsis of an object-relations theory of the personality. *The International Journal of Psychoanalysis, 44*(2), 224–5.

Freud, S. (1905). Three essays on the theory of sexuality. *SE 7*, 125–248.

Freud, S. (1920). Beyond the pleasure principle. *SE 18*, 3–66.

Freud, S. (1924). The economic problem of masochism. *SE 19*, 157–72.

Freud, S. (1926). Inhibitions, symptoms, and anxiety. *SE 20*, 77–178.

Freud, S. (1933a). Why war? *SE 22*, 197–218.

Freud, S. (1933b). New introductory lectures on psycho-analysis. *SE 22*, 3–184.

Freud, S. (1940). An outline of psycho-analysis. *SE 23*, 138–208.

Gabbard, G.O. (2000). Hatred and its rewards. *Psychoanalytic Inquiry, 20*, 409–20.

Giovacchini, P.L. (1990). Erotism and chaos. *Journal of the American Academy of Psychoanalysis, 18*(1), 5–17.

Grotstein, J.S. (1998). Discussion: Esther Sánchez-Pardo. *Gender and Psychoanalysis, 3*(1), 81–93.

Loewald, H.W. (1951). Ego and reality. *The International Journal of Psychoanalysis, 32*, 10–18.

Loewald, H.W. (1966). *Papers on psychoanalysis*. Yale University Press (1980).

Loewald, H.W. (1973). On internalization. *The International Journal of Psychoanalysis, 54*(1), 9–17.

Mahler, M.S., Pine, F., & Bergman, A. (1975). *The psychological birth of the human infant: Symbiosis and individuation*. Basic Books.

Renik, O. (1991). The biblical book of Job: Advice to clinicians. *Psychoanalytic Quarterly, 60*, 596–606.

Spitz, R.A. (1958). On the genesis of superego components. *Psychoanalytic Study of the Child, 13*, 375–404.

Stern, D.N. (1985). *The interpersonal world of the infant*. Basic Books.

Stoller, R.J. (1974). Hostility and mystery in perversion. *The International Journal of Psychoanalysis, 55*, 425–34.

Waelder, R. (2007). The principle of multiple function: Observations on over-determination. *Psychoanalytic Quarterly, 76*, 75–92.

Winnicott, D.W. (1953). Transitional objects and transitional phenomena – a study of the first not-me possession. *The International Journal of Psychoanalysis, 34*, 89–97.

Winnicott, D.W. (1965). *The maturational processes and the facilitating environment: Studies in the theory of emotional development.* The International Psycho-Analytical Library, 64. The Hogarth Press and the Institute of Psycho-Analysis.

Chapter 7

Inventing Oneself

The Effort Toward Self-Cure in a Psychotic Woman

The third bin is psychosis. I have very little clinical experience with the long-term intensive treatment of psychotically organized (or disorganized) patients, and I claim no expertise. I include this report for completeness and, I suppose, to get it off my chest. But it is, as Sherlock Holmes would say, not without interest. At the very least, it demonstrates the power of sadomasochism to hold people together, as described in the previous chapter. I find much more fondness in my heart for Yetta now than I did while I was working with her.

For 20 years I sat with and largely failed to understand this very disturbed but very courageous woman who was struggling to free herself from terror and despair. Gradually I have come to see how what she did in front of me (not so much *with* me) was an effort to design herself from the childhood ground up. I would like to describe the woman and the work as a reflection on how, in the absence of an effective capacity for repression or stable identifications, some people can use their conscious capacities in an attempt to replace or repair inadequate developmental processes.

Yetta was a profoundly isolated single woman who came to see me for therapy in her mid-fifties, about a year after the death of her previous therapist. She was the younger of two girls in a lower middle class blue-collar family. She had no social contacts, since she had retired from the waitressing job she had held for 30 years. She had intense feelings of despair, longed for love and marriage, but knew she could not sustain a relationship because she could not bear to be around other people. She had been happy with her last therapist, but his death interrupted the work after a few months. She had seen a number of therapists in her adult life, but only the first treatment had lasted over a year. That therapist was an alcoholic who kissed and fondled her. It is striking that she was able to say that what he did was wrong, "maybe even reportable to the psychiatric society," but that he was helpful to her until he lost his license. After we started, she had records sent to me; her previous therapists had diagnosed her as schizophrenic or schizoaffective.

DOI: 10.4324/9781003360391-9

In our first session she told me a dream and what she thought it meant. I then said, "I have some ideas about your dream too. Would you like to hear them?" (In retrospect, I am struck by the way I put it, as a question; I must have had an inkling of what was to come.) She responded simply, "No." In the year prior to seeing me she had interviewed 12 other therapists and had felt "abused" by all of them. One woman kept nodding sympathetically. "Why did she have to do that?" she asked rhetorically; she seemed to think it was self-evident that that was abuse. Other therapists kept insisting on interrupting her.

I somehow managed to avoid offending her and agreed to work with her, for reasons I continue to wonder about but certainly include my competitiveness with other practitioners, my inflated assessment of my own abilities, and my sadism. I had three hours a week available, which she accepted with some disappointment that I did not have any more. By the time I did have more hours available several months later, I declined to offer them to her because I was not sure I could bear more contact with her, and so we continued at three times a week.

We met face to face at first, but she was troubled when she could discern any reaction in my face, so she put herself on the couch. I tried to position myself so she could see me easily if she needed to (at the time I had a mistaken impression that she would lose needed contact with me otherwise), but she soon insisted that I move out of sight. She brought a raggedy teddy bear with her to each meeting. She also brought her own couch napkin and Kleenex.

Most of the meetings were monologues in which she would recount details of her parents' failures to love her (which for the most part seemed to be relatively ordinary selfishness, lapses of attention, or insensitivity) or her older sister's meanness. She would often speak in a babyish voice, which she described as "little me coming out." She would start to cry abruptly in mid-sentence, often for no discernible reason, and just as abruptly stop, without any acknowledgment. She had the specific understanding that her job was to remember and report every instance of masturbation in her life, apparently to rid herself of any sexual excitement. I do not know where she got the idea; it may have come from the first therapist. At any rate, she was convinced of it. As to the masturbation itself, two features recurred frequently: painful rubbing, and placing small objects in her vagina.

Soon into the work she revealed her expectations for the treatment: to marry and settle down in a loving relationship, and to compose music like Mozart. With respect to the latter, she had taken piano lessons, and she figured she had at least another 35 years to live, and Mozart had only lived 35 years, so if she started now then she could do it. She attributed her inability to compose music to her mental illness.

She would often punctuate her narrative mid-sentence with statements in the form of "And I don't want anyone [or sometimes, "Dr. G"] to do anything to my genitals [or vulva, or vagina, or anus]." These remarks came up several times per session, sometimes as the first thing she said, but even then starting with the word "and."

The First of Many Treatment Crises

At some point early on, I asked her to say more about something she was saying that I did not understand. She stopped, appeared agitated, and went into a tirade about my interrupting her and forcing her to think my thoughts instead of her own. I was silent for maybe a month after that, until I very tentatively asked her if it would be all right if I made a comment. She was just as disrupted by that remark as by the first. She made it clear that I was not to speak unless she invited me to. Every time I spoke, she would have an intensely negative reaction. Specifically, she would feel "raped." As best as I could discern, she was referring to a physical sensation of being penetrated. I learned much later that following such episodes she would feel terrified and suicidal. It would take her up to three months to get over the feelings, during which time she would make frequent references to "Dr. G's inability to control himself."

She always referred to me in the third person unless she was asking me a question; she did not talk to me, she talked in front of me. It seemed as if anything that came from me that was different from her expectations would provoke this reaction. For example, she asked me if I had heard of a link between cancer and B vitamins. When I answered "It doesn't ring a bell" instead of saying no, she reacted with rage, shouting about how I always have to hurt her. By the end of the second year, I had been restricted to speaking five words: yes, no, I don't know. Furthermore, for long stretches the only time she allowed me to speak was in answer to a rhetorical question, the form of which was "A mother shouldn't hate her daughter. Isn't that right, Dr. G?" It took me well into the third year to catch on to the literal extent that I was expected to adhere to these rules. Even so, 12 years after my last slip-up, she still referred to "Dr. G's inability to keep quiet" in the present tense.[1] She occasionally reminded me that she hates me for hurting her, and that she does not want to be like Dr. G.

She sometimes described the goal of our work as "having all the parts of myself together." By "parts" she meant specifically the father part, the mother part, the older sister part, and the "little me" part. She referred to their voices in her head, and she would point to the part of her head where each voice resided. The last time I disrupted her by speaking, she told me heatedly to "shut up." Then she repeated it in a faux male voice: "Shut up." She told me subsequently that she had been using her father's anger.

These failures of my self-control convinced Yetta that it was not safe to work the way she wanted with me. Although she was not explicit about what that meant (and I was not about to ask), two changes emerged at that time. First, she stopped speaking in a baby voice for the next ten years or so (the voice has come back occasionally since). Second, she introduced a new rhetorical habit. She would limit her narrative to almost nothing but a detailed description of her day-to-day plans, activities, diet and health, and her efforts to perfect them. She would follow stories of performing some household chore successfully with a statement that sounded like an implicit comparison of how she was acting contrasted to how her family members had failed to act, in the form of "If I had a daughter, I'd say, 'That's good that you keep your house clean, Yetta.'" (Note that she gave her "daughter" her own name.) In later years, these statements grew to "If I was a father and I had a daughter, or if I was a mother and I had a daughter, or if I was a big sister and I had a little sister, I'd say 'That's good that you ....'" She often jumbled up the nouns in the statement without noticing, e.g., "If I was a sister and I had a daughter." Occasionally she would add to the list, "or if I was a psychiatrist and I had a patient." I had the impression that she was trying to train her father/mother/sister parts.

Periodically she would tell me she hated me for making her work "this way," which had to do with doing things "out of order." It seemed that her idea was that she was not being allowed to start as a child and grow up because I had made it unsafe for "little me" to emerge.

Occasionally she would begin a session by saying that she had made a "mistake" in the previous hour, invariably having to do with one of those "If I had a daughter" statements. Upon further reflection, she had decided that what she would have said was not perfect, and she needed to correct it. For example, she announced that she had made a mistake by saying that if she had a daughter, she'd "give her a big hug and ...." She wasn't so sure that giving her daughter a hug would be appropriate. She was a perfectionist in many ways, in fact she seemed to be trying to use the therapy as an effort to think perfectly – which meant purifying her thoughts, apparently including ridding herself of sexual and aggressive feelings. Every thought was a potential misstep. In her day-to-day life she had to eat the perfect nutritional food (taste was not a consideration), take the perfect combination of vitamin supplements, walk 10,000 steps a day, and follow the perfect exercise regimen. If she had an ache or a pain, she assumed she had done something wrong psychologically; she was convinced that perfect mental health warded off all illness and aging.

Two Charged Memories

Yetta had many early memories that came up repeatedly, invariably as indictments of her parents or her sister, of which I will mention two. The first was a toilet training memory from her third year of life, reported with tears and barely controlled outrage. Her mother had put her on the potty and then turned the water on in the sink. It took several retellings of the incident before I understood that her perception of the event was that her mother was actually controlling her body with the water tap. The second may have been from age four or so, when she was bathing with her mother. She noticed her mother's pubic hair and asked her what it was. Her mother answered, "That means you're too old to be sharing a bath with me" – which she never did again. She added, "If I had a daughter, I'd say, 'Yetta, that's something you'll get when you're older.' I wouldn't punish her for being curious. I'd encourage her."

I sat silently with this woman three sessions a week for 20 years. During the monologues, I occasionally formulated to myself what I would tell her if I were allowed to tell her anything. For long stretches of time I alternated between feeling that I was chained to my chair as she tortured me and enjoying daydreams of her being killed in a traffic accident. Despite the fact that I felt I could easily have been replaced by a spool on a string, she had tremendous difficulty tolerating weekends or interruptions in our meetings. She was very explicit in saying so, sometimes describing it as another way "Dr. G" was injuring her, although she never expected or asked for any different arrangement.

After seven or eight years she began to improve symptomatically, to the point where she eventually developed a circle of casual friends and could find some simple pleasures in her life. She also developed some capacity for self-observation; she was eventually able to tell me that her intolerance of my speaking to her ("raping" her) had to do with the feeling that allowing another person's thoughts in her head meant being taken over by the speaker. Recently, thinking about how much she hates it when a therapist talks, she said, "If he talks, I'm afraid I'll lose myself." When she discovered that my office building was being sold, she wanted to have another therapist lined up for when I retired or died. It turned out that she had ruled out women therapists because she feared she would become a lesbian.

She never let me off the hook for speaking, but she has begun to think of this vulnerability as her problem and to hope she could advance to a point where she could tolerate other people's ideas.

Discussion

It is easily observed that in the course of normal development a preschool child will be relatively free with libidinal wishes and deeds, masturbating unashamedly and announcing her intention to marry both parents. Aggressive urges are also demonstrably at the forefront of her mental experience, e.g., in avowed intention and efforts to get rid of a younger sibling. The objects of her desire or destructiveness are family members above and before all others. It is also generally taken for granted (and in fact institutionalized by the educational system) that by the age of six or seven the preoccupation with sex and violence will have largely disappeared from awareness and the child will be able to direct her attention away from her family drama and onto the larger world. Freud (1923) described this as a movement from the phallic-oedipal phase to the latency period (p. 177). In a relatively brief period of time, what was available to the child's consciousness is rendered unconscious and kept that way. In the adult, a marker of this process having taken place successfully is infantile amnesia – the remarkable fact that, in relatively healthy adults, memories are more or less continuous going back to around age five or six but prior to that are only sporadic and typically function as screen memories.

Freud identified two aspects of the process by which major constituents of mental life are rapidly rendered unconscious: a massive repression and an identification with the parents, the latter being the major contributor to the formation of the superego.

One of the features of Yetta's case was that there was no obvious infantile amnesia. As far as I could tell, her memories were more or less continuous going back at least to toilet training. It seems that the earlier memories were less journalistically accurate and more stereotyped, but there was no discernible break in her recollections. It was also apparent in her adult life that her preoccupation with family dramas of sex and violence had either continued or reemerged since childhood. She dealt with frequent sexual thoughts by making statements that repudiated them ("And I don't want anyone to do anything to my genitals"). We can infer that she was not very good at maintaining repression.

Another feature of her case is the form in which she has taken in aspects of her family members – as physical presences in her head whom she can localize in space. This points to the nature and extent of her superego formation – as a committee of family members, rather than a personally owned capacity to judge (recall her using her father's voice to tell me to shut up). It also suggests why she has a sense of herself as an assortment of parts that need to be gathered together. As Freud (1923) pointed out, the ego, as well as the superego, is the "precipitate of abandoned object-cathexes" (p. 29). Her ego and superego are not fully internalized in the sense of taking on the traits of others and making them her own, but her "If I had a daughter" approach may be evidence of that work in progress. She is terrified of the influence of others, which she experiences as literally getting inside her head and changing or replacing her selected parts. At the same time, she has a quasi-psychoanalytic developmental theory that the route to change is to pick carefully the people (therapists) she spends time with because (unless she fights them off) she will end up being like them.

Loewald (1952) made the observation that the consequences of repression and those of internalization (e.g., the contributions of identifications to ego and superego formation) are very different. Repression locks down the wishes and fears of the moment in a way that fixes them, foreclosing any further maturation, whereas internalization ("structure building") processes are fluid, ongoing, and potentially creative. Of course, the virtue of repression is the relief from conscious preoccupation with one's impulses and the consequent availability of conscious processes for other tasks. It contributes to a mental "stimulus barrier." In Yetta's case, the inadequacy of repression leaves her with the requirement that she consciously repudiate every impulse she finds threatening.

The Effort to Invent Oneself

The observation I am making here is that, absent effective repression and stable identifications, Yetta finds herself in the position of trying to do defensive, adaptive, and developmental work with thoughts and feelings that she cannot keep out of her mind. This means that conscious judgment and the deployment of attention have to do the work that happens more or less automatically in normal childhood development. So her energies are devoted to the conscious invention of herself, on the model of being, first, her own mother, and subsequently her own father, older sister – and psychiatrist. I believe that, for the first few years at least, I interfered with that project; it was only late in the game that I began to get a glimmer of what she was doing. Ideally, perhaps I should have been saying the kind of things she now says to herself (following her implicit supervision of my work when she says "If I was a psychiatrist ..."). But I am not sure that would have been received any better than the things I did say, which felt to her as if I were forcing myself into her head. Recently she was able to say specifically what she wanted from a therapist: "to listen in compassionate silence."

What Am I, Chopped Liver?

I now need to recant the feeling I had earlier in the treatment that I could have been replaced by a spool on a string, as in the "fort-da" game. Although I cannot say exactly how, I am now convinced that my presence was a vital part of her improvement. Words like "witnessing" (Poland, 2000), "container/contained" (Bion, 1959), and "holding environment" (Winnicott, 1960) seem apt, but to me they seem more descriptive than explanatory. Winnicott (1962) once wrote that, as an analyst, he aimed at keeping alive, keeping well, and keeping awake (p. 166). I stayed alive and well, which was more than her last therapist could say. Staying awake was more of a challenge at times, but I managed.

She has put me to some use. The least I can say about it is that she benefitted from my ratifying her rhetorical questions ("Isn't that right, Dr. G?"). In retrospect, they were not exactly rhetorical after all. It seems that she granted me a temporary license to be a parent with whom she could then be a child. It was something akin to a situation I found myself in when my wife was in labor. I had left the room briefly, and when I returned she was agitated. I didn't know what to do until she said, "Tell me to relax!" I jumped right in and did so, and she relaxed – but at the time, she needed me to be the one with the voice of authority.

These thoughts about the process of change are very preliminary and very tentative. Certainly they raise more questions than they answer. I do know that I have changed with her; I notice a softer and more tolerant attitude in myself, along with an increasing respect for her courage. I think these changes mark a reduction in my own terror when confronted by the demons with which she lives.

The Syntax of Psychotic Mentation

I would like to underscore some aspects of how Yetta's mind works that I believe will be familiar to clinicians who study psychosis. Especially prominent is the concreteness of her thinking. Thoughts (and words) don't represent acts or things; they *are* acts or things. My words penetrated her and caused her physical pain. Her parents' voices resided in physical locations in her head. From her perspective, there was no "as if" quality, nothing metaphorical about those experiences. Here again the syntax reveals the ontology.

As a related matter: Freud's (1923) observation that the ego is "first and foremost a body-ego" (p. 27) is borne out here; her experience of her own mind is as a bodily organ that needs to be strengthened by purification and exercise, in the form of (concretely) incorporating verbal parental advice – or, rather, incorporating her perfected self-as-parent giving advice.

Finally, let us note the confusion between herself and others in those self-administered doses of parental wisdom. Along with her sense of inevitably becoming like her analyst, whomever that may be, we see her experience of being porous, of not being fully differentiated from others.

Yetta continued to improve. Her perfectionism in her self-invention remained fierce, but she began to entertain a more nuanced view of the world: "If I had a mother [etc.], I'd say, 'People aren't perfect, they are all a mix of good and bad, and you can get along with the good and ignore the bad.'" Her last reported discovery was that there are degrees of badness: "Murder is very bad, and lying is bad, but not as bad as murder, and hurting someone's feelings through insensitivity isn't as bad. Isn't that right, Dr. G?"

Yes.

Note

1   One of the consequences of the rule of silence was that even now I know precious little of her history.

References

Bion, W.R. (1959). Attacks on linking. *The International Journal of Psychoanalysis, 40*, 308–15.

Freud, S. (1923). The ego and the id. *SE 19*, 1–66.

Loewald, H.W. (1952). The problem of defense and the neurotic interpretation of reality. *The International Journal of Psychoanalysis, 33*, 444–9.

Poland, W.S. (2000). The analyst's witnessing and otherness. *Journal of the American Psychoanalytic Association, 48*(1), 17–34.

Winnicott, D.W. (1960). The theory of the parent-infant relationship. *International Journal of Psychoanalysis, 41*, 585–95.

Winnicott, D.W. (1962). *The maturational processes and the facilitating environment.* International Universities Press (1965).

Chapter 8

Neurotic, Perverse, and Psychotic Action

The analytic encounter has two dimensions: action and reflection. Historically, our literature has emphasized the reflective conclusions of the analyst about the patient's "narrative" – that is, on what the patient has to say. The analyst's participation was limited – at least in the clinical reports – to statements of inference about the patient. More contemporary literature has begun to take seriously the fact that the analysts, even after being analyzed, still have unconscious wishful and fearful motives; that is to say, they remain human. As Merton Gill once put it, you can still recognize your friends after they have been analyzed.

Given the fact that the analyst's mind follows the same psychological rules as the patient's, it makes sense to see the "text" to be analyzed as an ongoing interactive drama with two authors and two actors playing multiple roles. Periodically, either or both can become reviewers and reflect on the action; that is the interpretive work. Reflection on one aspect of the action doesn't stop the action; interpretive action often takes the form of simultaneously enacting what is being interpreted. Imagine, for example, an analyst saying to a patient, with an evident sense of triumph, "We seem to be caught up in a power struggle." At other times, the interpretive moment will enact a different scene that remains to be discovered.

Analytic listening thus addresses two questions: What is the patient saying? And what are we doing as we have this conversation? The traditional listening to the narrative is still necessary, but it needs to be taken in the context of the interactive drama. Simply put, actions speak louder than words. We draw two kinds of inferences from what the patient shows us in action: One is the syntax of the patient's thought, and the other is the nature of the drama.

The action involves both actors in the drama. But just as there are a few useful generalities that can be formulated about the patients as members of a "bin" independently of the therapist, each bin involves characteristic ways of putting pressure on the therapist to accept a role.

DOI: 10.4324/9781003360391-10

Neurotic Action

Of the three broad categories, the action in neurosis is the most varied and nuanced because the neurotic appreciates that she is dealing with an actual independent person in the analyst. Thus, the action is enriched with – and complicated by – compliance based on the capacity for empathy. Neurotic symptomatology begins with inhibited and disguised desires. Thus, the pressure on the analyst to accept a role is typically subtler with neurotic patients than with others. It is facile – and not very informative – to say that the drama enacted will be an oedipal one. A more useful generalization might be that the analyst will be cast as the voice of the patient's conscience, as personified by interactions with one parent or the other. Thus, the therapist often finds herself in the position of being permissive or restrictive.

This is not to say that the drama simply reenacts a scene from the patient's past, no matter what the therapist does. I think it would be more correct to say that the patient sees something in the therapist that confirms her view of a whole class of people – either men or women – and tries to exploit it in the present. If the analyst has sufficient familiarity with the trait the patient has detected, and sufficient distance to bear it, she will eventually be able to make it, and its underlying assumptions, the subject of attention. Otherwise, the action will include either the analyst's unconscious acceptance or rejection of the assigned role. In this sense the beginning of interpretive work is often the patient's perception of a trait in the analyst, rather than the other way around.

Perverse Action

Perverse action is easier to describe than neurotic action, because it is less nuanced and more obvious. Interactions are typically sadomasochistic, and they are not muted by either empathy or realistic judgment. The perverse patient acts as if the world were as she wished it, which puts tremendous pressure on the therapist to comply or to confront. The action will be based on the patient's undisguised premise that she is not supposed to suffer, and therefore any discomfort in the patient is evidence that the analyst is a torturer.

One of the typical unconscious motivations for becoming a therapist is the desire to see suffering and to prove we are not the cause of it. Thus analysts are particularly vulnerable to the insistence that we are torturers. It is likely to provoke the analyst to strike back, or to go overboard to soothe the patient, in a kind of masochistic submission. This is the reason the term "borderline" (and perhaps the term "perverse") is used pejoratively. This group of patients provokes the strongest negative reactions among most analysts.

Another aspect of the action comes from the unwillingness of these patients to accept unwanted implications. Work that seems deepening one day will have disappeared the next. This protective disavowal by the patient has the additional effect of torturing the therapist by conveying the message that the therapist cannot do anything to help. This also puts pressure on the therapist to do something sadistic to make the helplessness go away, or to surrender masochistically.

The relentless pressure on the therapist to be something other than a therapist also has a beneficial effect: The patient makes it almost impossible for the analyst to avoid noticing her participation in the action. This was particularly challenging to American mainstream analysts beginning around 1970, who began seeing more perversely organized ("widening scope") patients in analysis, but whose theories depicted the analyst as not participating in the action at all, other than interpreting. That was the era in which the term "borderline" was coined.

Psychotic Action

Psychotic action is the most stereotyped of all, in the sense that the issues seem without shading or nuance. The analyst may be treated as a nonhuman object or as an allegorical figure, but underlying the action is the blurred distinction between self and other. In the previous chapter, Yetta treated me as a witness who was bound and gagged like Bobby Seale in the Chicago Eight trial. My more active participation, i.e., speaking aloud, was experienced as a physical and sexual assault. Psychotic patients are less likely to provoke sadomasochistic reactions in the analyst as intense as those provoked by perverse patients, because their idiosyncrasies of thought provide some automatic distance. In other words, the analyst is less likely to feel like a torturer, or to feel tortured, because it is easier to see the patient as an alien. It is also easier for the therapist to accept her limits and cut the work short, or take a nonanalytic "management" approach to therapy.

From my limited experience, I imagine the analyst who genuinely engages with a psychotic patient is likely to feel either crazy or dead, by virtue of the incomplete self-object differentiation of the patient. For the patient, there is only one subject in the room, and the analyst is either a part of it, or she does not exist.

In this section I have put forth my minimalist approach to diagnosis and my sketches of the shape of action with people in each category. I have gone about as far as (or maybe a little farther than) I am comfortable in generalizing about the people we work with. In the next section I will turn to what we do when we do what we do.

Part II

What Do We Do When We Do What We Do?

When beginning analytic candidates come to us with their first training cases, having already been immersed in analytic theory, they often beseech us: "I know all that, but what do I *do* with the patient?" Very few are satisfied with the answer, "Just listen," or "Trust your instincts." Listening, it turns out, is complicated and unnatural, especially when you are anxious. Besides listening *to*, one has to learn to listen *for*, and to listen *with*. And our instincts terrify us.

Candidates are often afraid they will hurt someone if they make a misstep. Sometimes we offer them rules, especially about what not to do. The rules don't actually mean very much, but they do make both analyst and supervisor feel less helpless. When the candidate is calm enough to listen, then we can listen to how they listen and help them use who they are.

In this section I begin with the relatively simple observation that one can infer something about the degree to which patients "own"[1] their problems from the syntax of their presentation. Somewhat to my surprise I found that candidates loved the idea of using it for case selection and evaluation. I suspect this is not so much because it is such a valuable idea, but rather that it gave them a way to organize and contain their anxiety about starting with someone new – in effect, it said: "Here is a way you can listen." In Chapter 10, I briefly take up the problem of how language obscures as it reveals.

Beginning with Chapter 11, I try to address what we are actually doing when we do what we do. Here I begin to take up a theme that runs through the rest of Part II and Part III, which is the discontinuity between what we think we do (our explicit theories) and what we actually do (our underlying, often unconscious convictions as revealed in our clinical actions), starting by noticing the vast array of noninterpretive ways we influence our patients. In Chapter 12 I argue for the centrality of acknowledging and tolerating one's own ignorance in the clinical situation. In Chapter 13 I further develop the thesis that the important differences between analysts have more to do with their characters than with their theories.

DOI: 10.4324/9781003360391-11

Note

1   For an elegant discussion of "owning," see Shengold (1995).

Reference

Shengold, L. (1995). *Delusions of everyday life*. Yale University Press.

Chapter 9

The Syntax of the Presenting Complaint

Mistakes were made.

(Ronald Reagan)

In a paper on patients' theories of pathogenesis, Steven Goldberg (1991) reported on two patients who entered analysis with fixed ideas about the nature of their own difficulties. Goldberg showed how these ideas served the patients' defensive and communicative purposes. In one case, Ms. A came in for problems in relationships with men, which Goldberg was quickly able to understand as her strongly held conscious conviction that her problems stemmed from the fact that men, beginning with her father, had mistreated her (Goldberg, 1991, p. 254). In the other case, Ms. B also sought treatment to improve her relations with men, which she insisted was a result of her father's regarding her as unworthy (Goldberg, 1991, p. 260).

It occurred to me that the syntax of the patients' ideas had a particular form: "My problem is that my father mistreated me" (Ms. A); and "My problem is that my father regarded me as unworthy" (Ms. B). The two case examples, chosen because the patients clung so tenaciously to their theories, seem very similar, and the theories themselves seem almost identical. I imagine that most practitioners would immediately note the externalization of the theories. But the externalizing quality was imbedded in the syntax of the statements, in particular the passive voice. This led me to wonder what inferences could be drawn about others who come for treatment from the syntax of their complaints when framed in terms of their preferred, conscious theories of pathogenesis. I have come to the conclusion that, in an initial consultation, the analyst can usually find or construct a statement (as Goldberg did) that conveys the patient's consciously held views, and that the syntax of the statement of the presenting complaint when rephrased in light of those views will fall into one of four categories. We may put them in this form: "My problem is that ..."

DOI: 10.4324/9781003360391-12

1. I *do something* that I don't want to do;
2. I *am something* that I don't want to be;
3. I *have* a condition that I don't want to have;
4. Someone has *done something to me*.

I suggest that the syntactical categories have some prognostic use and attention to the categories has heuristic value in training situations. In what follows I will give brief illustrations of each category, then consider some inferences that might be drawn from them.

1. *"I do." Assistant Professor Plum* came for a consultation for help with anxiety related to his upcoming review for tenure. As part of the review, his university required him to provide a list of scholars in his field who could comment on the quality of his work. He noted that he kept putting off contacting his colleagues. When I asked why, he said he was afraid that they might not think highly of his work. He offered spontaneously, "But I know that doesn't make sense. These are collaborators I've known forever. I already know they respect my work." When I asked what happened when he tried to make the calls, he described how he would get nervous, his heart would race, his palms would sweat "as if I was asking them out on a date," and he would stop before he began.

   At this point we can already craft a statement with which the patient would agree, expressing the presenting complaint: "I put off doing something I want to do because it makes me anxious, for reasons I don't understand."

2. *"I am." Sgt. Mustard* was referred by a friend who was concerned about his mood. When we met he told me he was having trouble reintegrating into civilian life after his years in the military. I asked in what way. He said, "I'm depressed," as if it were an explanation. He described a withdrawal from daily activities, to the point that he rarely left his house. I found I had to ask a lot of questions to elicit information, but I was able to piece together that he was sleeping adequately, his appetite and sexual interest was unaffected, and he still enjoyed a variety of activities, once he got to them. When I asked what kept him from, for example, going to the batting cages as he used to, he "explained" again: "I'm depressed." Eventually he was able to agree that he got anxious when he took action, but since he wasn't taking any at present, he felt no anxiety. He did not see that as a problem, much less one that he had any interest in exploring. Further discussion confirmed that he felt his situation was unchangeable, and he had come to see me only to satisfy his friend.

   In this example our statement is a direct quote: "I'm depressed." The self-diagnosis rationalized his inhibitions and his passivity.

3. *"I have." Ms. Peacock* also told me she came in because "I'm depressed." When I tried to pursue the question of what she was experiencing, she cut

me off abruptly, explaining, "Depression is a biological condition. You're a doctor. I'm not interested in exploring my childhood, I just want you to give me medication."

In this instance, although she used the same words Sgt. Mustard had used, Ms. Peacock meant something different. It was not exactly that she *was* depressed; rather, she was saying that she *had* a condition called depression.

4. *"Someone has done something to me."* Goldberg's (1991) cases are perfect illustrations: "My father mistreated me." Here is a more extreme example: *Mr. Green* was an inpatient in a psychiatric hospital during my residency. He had agreed to be interviewed by a senior attending psychiatrist in front of the group, for teaching purposes. The interviewer asked him why he was in the hospital. He responded calmly and thoughtfully, "It happens that I am being pursued across the city by a giant rat."

The Nature of the Categories

I have listed the categories in descending order of "ownership" of the problem: *I do, I am, I have, something was done to me.*

1. *I do ...* This first category tends to imply recognition of the problem as self-created, and it is music to the analyst's ears. Prof. Plum was already prepared to see himself as the author of his own difficulties and to join in the search for unrecognized motivation. His syntax demonstrates a capacity for self-observation and readiness to entertain the existence of an unconscious mental life. The prospects for analytic work seem good. That is not to say we know what the patient will do with it, or how superficial or compliant the statement may prove to be. But, absent other information, it is the most encouraging way the prospective patient could begin to see his difficulties. We might compare this category to Zetzel's (1968) "true hysteric" who sought treatment because it was "clear to her that the problem [lay] within herself" (p. 258).[1]

The syntactical forms "I can't," "I won't," and "I don't" might be considered subtypes of this category, or perhaps a short step further down the ladder, depending on how easily the patient accepts the translation into a definitive action. For example, Prof. Plum might have said, "I can't make myself do ...," but he would have had no difficulty accepting the translation to "you put off doing ...." For others, the negative is more important: As Schafer[2] (1973) pointed out, "can't" implies being out of one's control, "won't" implies willfulness, and "don't" is descriptively neutral (pp. 263–4). Each of these would need to be opened up to formulate accurately in terms of the patient's theory of pathogenesis.

When I coined the statement for Prof. Plum, I added the phrase "[I do it] for reasons I don't understand." Prof. Plum knows that there is something important he does not yet know. This is in marked contrast to Goldberg's cases, both of which were selected to highlight the defensive use of a theory of pathogenesis. In other words, they had to believe they already knew where the problem lay, and it was not within themselves. This insistence on a kind of certainty is shared in varying degree by all the categories except the first.

2. *I am ...* This category corresponds to what Sartre (1965) called "bad faith" (*mauvaise foi*), or self-deception, in his writing about existential psychoanalysis (p. 182). It amounts to viewing oneself as an unchanging thing. By defining himself as depressed, Sgt. Mustard took refuge from his anxiety about what he might do or become if he were to see himself as an agent rather than as fixed in an unchanging state. The therapeutic task at the outset would have to include addressing the function of his doing so – that is, to show him that he is acting in a meaningful way by trying to portray himself as not doing anything. The actual Sgt. Mustard was able to work with that, though some patients cling more stubbornly to the claim that they cannot change anything. The syntactical form implies an effort to have the therapist accept the *status quo*.

3. *I have ...* In contrast to Sgt. Mustard's "I am" depressed, Ms. Peacock's "I have depression" implies an even further remove, one in which the problem is not what she *does*, nor who she *is*, but a foreign body, a "not me" that she *has*. In her mind, the appropriate treatment is akin to surgical excision and should not require her participation. The task of the evaluation would be to see if she can be engaged in reconsidering and, if not, to shift therapeutic gears away from the analytic or make the appropriate referral. The prognosis for analytic work in the traditional sense is not encouraging. In the actual case on which Ms. Peacock is based, there was no second session. But there is considerable variation in this group.

4. *Someone has done something to me ...* This formulation is about as far as one can go from the source of a problem while still acknowledging something is wrong. It is what we mean when we use the term externalization. In contrast to Ms. Peacock, who at least acknowledged being the container of the problem, Mr. Green's problem just kept following him. The prognosis for participating constructively in an analytic therapy is probably the lowest in this group, but one can always be surprised. When Mr. Green was being interviewed, the psychiatrist asked him at one point, "Did you ever consider the possibility that the rat was something inside you?" Mr. Green responded, "What, you mean like memories, or feelings and such?" I think the interviewer was as stunned as the rest of us at that moment, though he managed to say, "Well, yes, that's exactly what I mean." But by the end of the interview the rat was back on the streets.

Discussion

It is worth emphasizing that, when I suggest considering the syntax of the complaint, it is not identical with what the patient actually says. It is instead the analyst's construction based on what he can learn quickly about the patient's conscious theory of pathogenesis. We can be wrong, and we often are. A patient who, like Goldberg's two cases, complains that she can't make a go of a romantic relationship may say it is because "I always choose inappropriate men" — a statement that sounds like our first and prognostically best category. But we may discover that what she means to convey is that each man failed her — and the complaint may transpose into those of Goldberg's patients: I choose badly "because my father mistreated me."

Similarly, a patient who came to me saying "I'm afraid of intimacy" (Ellen, discussed in the next chapter) went on to explain that a previous therapist had told her that her anxiety in social situations was "just" her fear of intimacy. From the context I would have constructed a statement in the form of "I *have* a fear of intimacy" — an idea that she used to foreclose further exploration. On the other side of the coin, a man whose spoken complaint was "Nobody cuts me any slack" was readily able to recognize that he *treated* others as if they did not matter to him.

It is also important to stress that the issue is not the accuracy of the patient's theories, but rather the use to which the theory is put. Consider, for example, a common presentation of people who have been sexually abused as children. Such people's *spoken* complaints typically fall into our fourth syntactical category; that is, they often vehemently insist that their problems were caused by what was done to them by the abuser, adding that their participation was coerced and completely unpleasant.

It is easy to see that they are substantially correct about the abuse, that the responsibility *in childhood* lay with the adult(s) — although unconsciously they seem not to believe it. The evaluation of such people for analytic treatment may well turn on the question of whether the patient can entertain the possibility that she seems to be answering an internal accusation. If so, the analyst may be able to infer a more encouraging statement, for example "I can't seem to let go of the past events" — a category one version that implies some ownership of the present difficulties, or, more modestly, "I'm damaged goods," a category two statement.

The syntactical categories suggested here do not in any way replace any aspect of the evaluation for treatment. Nor are they infallible prognostic indicators. I have already given examples of how the phrasing of the presenting complaint and the assessment of the patient's preferred theory of pathogenesis are inferential and subject to error or revision. What they do provide is a hint, particularly for the clinician in training, about how to listen and generate hypotheses. Perhaps their greatest clinical value will prove to be in the negative: If the analyst cannot formulate a sentence for the patient's complaint that includes the patient's actions (our category one), that should at least raise a red flag about the patient's capacity to join in an analytic search for unconscious motivation.

We might note in passing that, despite the earlier comparison with Zetzel's "true hysteric," the syntactical categories do not directly correspond to traditional diagnostic categories. Mr. Green, for example, was psychotic; yet if he had been able to sustain an appreciation of the "rat" being his own creation, the prognosis for an interpretive therapy would have been more encouraging. And we have all interviewed neurotic patients who, like Ms. Peacock, clung adamantly to the insistence that their problem be considered only from a biological perspective.

The goal of this contribution is not to give answers but to provide another tool to help us notice, so we can raise the right questions. What I have described is done automatically by experienced clinicians. I hope these ideas will both alert the younger clinician to another element of listening and contribute to the discussion about what we are doing when we are listening.

Notes

1 Zetzel (1968) also lists four categories of patients in descending order of suitability for analysis, but, with the exception of the quotation, she defines her categories by underlying pathology.
2 Although attention to language is a hallmark of psychoanalytic listening, no one in the English language literature has made a larger or more systematic study of language and syntax in the clinical setting than Roy Schafer.

References

Goldberg, S.H. (1991). Patients' theories of pathogenesis. *The Psychoanalytic Quarterly,* 60(2), 245–75.
Sartre, J.P. (1965). *Essays in existentialism* (J. Wahl, Trans.). Citadel Press.
Schafer, R. (1973). The idea of resistance. *The International Journal of Psychoanalysis,* 54(3), 259–85.
Zetzel, E.R. (1968). The so called good hysteric. *The International Journal of Psychoanalysis,* 49(2–3), 256–60.

Chapter 10

An Observation on Naming and Language

The single biggest problem in communication is the illusion that it has taken place.
(Attributed to George Bernard Shaw)

In her description of the child's development of language to describe feelings, Anny Katan (1961) noted especially the function of speech to increase control over affects and drives. She reasoned that having words for feelings made judgment possible and that speech, as "trial action" (Freud, 1911), interposed a delay between thinking and action that helped avoid future impulsivity and "acting out."[1]

A recent observation of a small boy and his mother brought Katan's view to mind and suggested another way in which words help to control experience. It also started a train of thought that took me to a different station. It made me consider one of the functions of naming in particular and of verbal language in general.

Ben

Ben, a boy of eighteen months of age, was playing actively on the sidewalk when he fell and skinned his elbow. He stood up and howled, it seemed to me in outrage as much as in pain, his arms at his side, his eyes on the sky. His mother had been watching, and she could see the scrape on his elbow. As she approached him, she said in a voice more soothing than concerned, "Oh, poor Ben, you hurt your elbow." After she said that, he put his hand over the injured elbow.

It struck me that, by naming the injury, Ben's mother circumscribed it. It was not a global disaster; it was a sore elbow. The name served to isolate the experience, to sequester it as the immune system would wall off a foreign body. Once named, it stopped *happening* and became a *type* of experience.

DOI: 10.4324/9781003336039-13

Ellen

Ben and his mother put me in mind of a young woman I mentioned briefly in the last chapter. Ellen had just moved from another city, interrupting her analysis. She came to see me, hoping to continue her treatment. As she told me about her reasons for seeing her former analyst, she mentioned that she had been painfully shy. "But Dr. B told me it was just my fear of intimacy, and I'm doing better now."

I was struck by the word *just*. It implied that there was nothing more to think about. Dr. B had given her permission to be intimate and also to stop thinking about it. The "just" was implicit in Ben's mother's reaction as well: It was just his elbow, not his life. Ellen's anxious *experience* was replaced by a *category* of experiences called fear of intimacy.

In a classic paper, Glover (1931) described what he called inexact interpretations and explored how they could have therapeutic, but not analytic, benefits. Dr. B's interpretation is a case in point; she provided her patient with an obsessional defense – isolation – by using her transference authority to manage, rather than explore, her patient's anxiety. Naming an experience distances the subject from it.

And what of verbal language in general? As chair of a panel, Smith (1997) observed, "We can see how quickly [the panelists] are 'talking past each other,' even when they appear at moments to be in agreement. I am suggesting that this apparent confusion of tongues has resulted in part from fundamentally different and not wholly conscious readings and identifications with past figures" (p. 338).

"Identifications with past figures" – in a word, transferences – influence every human interaction, certainly those including conversation. But, more fundamentally, verbal language itself is an imprecise map of experience, and the map is not the territory. Our common-sense understanding of language is that it facilitates communication, but it does so in part *by virtue of its imprecision*. A map oversimplifies the territory to make it understandable. Language turns unique experiences into classes, then manipulates the classes. In short, it papers over differences between people and creates the *illusion* of understanding.

This is not an argument for solipsism. I do believe people experience a shared understanding in certain remarkable nonverbal experiences, including encounters with art or partaking of the sacrament of Communion. I suspect, following Loewald (1972), that the prototype of such experiences is the predifferentiated infant–mother nursing dyad. Moreover, I think analysis, as extended conversation, uses language – in the form of self-correcting recursive dialogue – to approach shared understanding asymptotically. But once naming takes hold, words begin to mediate experience. Much is gained, but something is lost as well.

In clinical work we have all had patients who talk a good analytic game, only to unravel when faced with termination. With them, it is easy to see in retrospect how language was being used defensively to sound like analytic work. Even more obvious is the patient who manipulates verbal concepts with facility, but if you ask what the patient is picturing, the response is "I wasn't picturing anything; I was thinking." Speaking is a meaningful action, but the content of the words obscures its meaning as often as it reveals it. It is a truth known to all analysts that the action speaks louder than the words.

We have to entertain the notion that words *always* have an isolating function, and that analytic work *always* involves trying to get past the words. We do so by studying and engaging with the action, the evocation, the encounter. The analysis of transference is not the study of what the patient *says* about the analyst, but rather what we infer the patient to be *doing* with us.

We work around the language by encouraging "free association" – that is, by inviting something like "automatic speech," analogous to Yeats's (1929) automatic writing. Or, in the Sullivanian tradition, we do so by "detailed inquiry" (Levenson, 1991), in which the analyst requires the patient to spell out every abstraction or allusion until the patient's selective inattention is foiled. Or we do it with silence, leaving patients to listen to what they just said.

But analysis is interpretation, and we tend to think of interpretation as spoken words. I remember a moment from my training analysis when my analyst had said something that did not impress me. I responded, "You have a voice like a cello, but you have absolutely nothing to say." I was more affected by his voice than by his words. Our literature has become more sophisticated in its appreciation of the role of nonverbal communication in analysis, but we still write as if interpretation means a pithy sentence or two whose meaning opens up the patient's awareness. I would prefer to say analysis proceeds by cooperative interpretive work – the interaction of perspectives – rather than by punch lines spoken by the analyst.

Language – beginning with naming – is categorizing; it translates from the particular to the general. That is the mind's part of the analytic work (some might say the analytic part). But the heart's part is the intense, lived experience of the analytic couple that defies language. Speech is made comprehensible by the omission of detail. This means that all speech obscures as well as communicates.

Note

1 See also Greenacre (1950).

References

Freud, S. (1911). Formulations regarding the two principles of mental functioning. SE *10*, 213–25.

Glover, E. (1931). The therapeutic effect of inexact interpretation: A contribution to the theory of suggestion. *The International Journal of Psychoanalysis, 12*, 397–411.

Greenacre, P. (1950). General problems of acting out. *The Psychoanalytic Quarterly,* *19,* 455–67.

Katan, A. (1961). Some thoughts about the role of verbalization in early childhood. *The Psychoanalytic Study of the Child, 16,* 184–8.

Levenson, E.A. (1991). *The purloined self.* William Alanson White Institute.

Loewald, H.W. (1972). The experience of time. *The Psychoanalytic Study of the Child,* 27, 401–10.

Smith, H.F. (1997) Creative misreading: Why we talk past each other. *Journal of the American Psychoanalytic Association, 45*(2), 335–57.

Yeats, W.B. (1929). *A packet for Ezra Pound.* Cuala Press.

Chapter 11

The Analyst's Influence

In our effort to distinguish psychoanalysis from other therapies, we have tended to emphasize the role of interpretive influence in bringing about therapeutic change. Analysis is interpretation. But the wish to differentiate what is analytic from what is "merely suggestion" has led to a relative disregard (at least in our theorizing) of the role of influences that, although not unique to analysis, are nonetheless essential for making an analytic process possible. In some circles the centrality of interpretation has become the ideal of technique to the extent that all other influences are viewed as contaminants of the process.

It should be apparent that in analysis, as in any human interaction, each person is constantly influencing the other; what else, after all, could "interaction" mean? So the question for analysts is not *whether* to influence patients in noninterpretive ways, but how best to be aware of those influences and put them to good analytic use.

In this chapter I would like to take a look at a moment of ordinary analytic work in an effort to call attention to some of the influences the analyst brings to bear in the course of the work. I believe they will be recognizable to all clinicians, although as analysts we tend not to emphasize them in our theorizing. I hope to raise the question: What kinds of influence are necessary to establish the conditions for an analytic process, i.e., for shared interpretive work to take place? Among the other questions this may include are: What is the nature of the analyst's authority to influence the patient to undertake such an unlikely enterprise as psychoanalysis? What influence is brought to bear in establishing a therapeutic alliance? What is the role of the analyst's authority as an expert? What is the role of transference authority? And, finally, how does the analyst influence the patient to question the analyst's transference authority?

Clinical Example

A man in his third year of analysis began the hour by handing me a check, as expected. I noticed, and pointed out, that he had underpaid by the amount

DOI: 10.4324/9781003360391-14

of one hour's fee. He immediately recognized the error and became incensed. "Money is your priority," he complained, beginning a protracted diatribe about my interest in the money, and how it proved I did not really care about him.

Eventually, I commented that his being so upset about what *I* had done helped him keep from considering the meaning of what *he* had done. In a more subdued if begrudging tone, he began to talk about his mistake with the check. He had canceled an hour during the month. He had not wanted to pay for it, although he knew our agreement obligated him to do so. He had also not wanted to make an issue of it; he had the idea that I might fight back, and he did not want to deal with my angry reaction. He added that he knew I had done nothing to warrant his suspicion.

I then commented on his readiness to dismiss his suspicions of me, and I suggested that we consider the possibility that he had seen something in me that he was eager to overlook. With considerable reluctance, he revealed that he had noticed certain habits – rituals, really – that I had developed for dealing with his payment. He had surmised (correctly) that I was trying to handle some uneasiness I had about the transactions. More important, he had concluded (also correctly, I realized later) that I did not want either of us to notice my uneasiness. He had anticipated my being angry in a confrontation about money because he surmised that I would be upset about being exposed. Subsequent associations led him to reconsider certain aspects of his dealings with his father, with whom he fought passionately, but whose characteristic patterns of dishonesty he managed to overlook.

Interpretive Influence

To begin with, I would like to consider my last two comments and their influence. Without getting into the very important and thorny question of what is and what is not an interpretation, I think most would agree that by most definitions they were in the *form* of interpretations. I am not suggesting that these were the only possible interpretations, or that they were good interpretations, or even that my observations were correct; I am only asserting that they were interpretations, and as such they were designed to influence the patient by their content, to notice what he had failed (or tried not) to notice, in order to expand his self-awareness. This confrontation with a new perspective, whether it is provided by the analyst or by the patient, is what I understand to be interpretive influence.

The patient's response to these comments would seem to confirm that they were successful in so influencing him. In the first instance, he recognized that there were motives of his own he was shouting down with his passionate reaction to me; his subsequent recall and elaboration of the passionate fights with his father threw further light on the meaning of this kind of interaction. In the second instance, he confirmed that he had tried to disavow certain perceptions of me that threatened to be the harbingers of more potentially disturbing interactions and realizations: He did not want to face any sign of my corruptibility, out of the conviction that our relationship depended on his overlooking it. Note, by the way, that, although it reminded him of his father's more threatening dishonesty, it was not simply a "distortion" or a "projection" but rather an accurate perception of something I did that had personal significance for him. Gill (1982) has often reminded us that transference reactions are reactions to real situations.

Noninterpretive Influence

If we understand the impact of these interpretations in the (admittedly schematic) traditional way, we would note that the patient was influenced by the sense of the analyst's interpretations to notice what heretofore he had managed not to notice. This is what we expect of "tactful," "properly timed," "correct" interpretations. In passing, we should note that every one of these modifiers raises a new set of questions about influence. Tact, or the lack of it, is a powerful noninterpretive influence, the nature of which has been barely touched on in our literature, save for one elegant paper by Poland (1975). Timing, good or bad, is another form of noninterpretive influence.

Correctness, or incorrectness, is one we have considered before – although the most provocative paper in the literature on the subject is over 90 years old. Glover's (1931) paper on the effect of "inexact" interpretation, which was subtitled "A Contribution to the Theory of Suggestion," is germane. Even so, it remains to be clarified what "correctness" actually means. Glover himself seemed to believe that correct interpretations would eliminate the role of noninterpretive influence in analysis. Levenson (1991) has gone so far as to suggest that the "correctness" of an interpretation is not very important.

Apart from any question of whether the two interventions under consideration were correct, tactful, and timely, their impact is certainly not limited to those facts. As Levenson (1991), Gill (1991), and others have pointed out, an interpretation is also an interaction. This implies that other, noninterpretive influences are brought to bear on the patient whenever an interpretation is made.

Consider the first comment. The patient revealed in response that he had anticipated my angry reaction. In retrospect, it was clear to me that I was irritated by the patient's underpayment, and also that I was uneasy with his angry reaction to my bringing it up. I believe that among my motives for making the interpretation, along with an effort to help him understand what I had noticed about him and pointed out, was the wish to distract him from his anger, and the wish to get him to talk about the money. The patient had read my comment as a sign of my intolerance of awareness of my own problems about money, and (for the most part) he sought to accommodate me. In any case, whatever my motives, I believe my intervention directed the patient to stop being angry at me and start talking about himself, and he complied. As R.D. Laing (1965) might have said, he knew better than to know what he knows he is not supposed to know.

When I called the patient's attention to his error, it is clear I made a choice by acting at that moment, a choice that revealed I thought the patient's mistake was more important than what he had begun to talk about. Not incidentally, this choice was consistent with the patient's perception of me as being overly interested in money. Then, when I elected to comment on the patient's bluster, I made another choice from among several options. I could have addressed the affect he was keeping out of awareness rather than the action; from previous work I had good reason to suspect that he was ashamed and frightened of his error, both for its meaning as withholding and for its significance as an uncontrolled spillage from inside him. Or I could have encouraged the elaboration of his picture of me or pursued any of the particulars, all presumably significant, that I neglected even to mention in my summary.

It may be argued that one or another of these approaches would have been more profitable, or less "countertransference motivated," and that may be so. What I am trying to emphasize is that *any* interpretation also enacts something and thus influences the patient in ways that far exceed the content of the words. My action was influential, not because I interpreted "the" issue, but because I made choices about what issue I thought was important from a variety of motives – some altruistic, some selfish, some reasoned, some irrational, some available to my awareness, some not – and, more generally, because I took a position that could not help but have an impact. The interpretive moment was also a "countertransference enactment" (Renik, 1993a) – as I believe *every* interpretation must be (see Part III).

In the second instance, I invited the patient to reflect on what he had noticed about me. This helped bring the enactment into the analytic part of the work by making it thematic. At the same time, it is likely that I conveyed to the patient my openness to hearing his perceptions of me that made it easier for him to face them. This is not a "neutral" stance; it is a position that carries a promise that I will behave in a way that is perhaps startlingly contrary to the patient's expectations. My interpreting thus enacts something else at the same time – in this instance, something reassuring. My unexpected response, though not an interpretive *statement*, was part of the interpretive work; it facilitated the patient's recognition of his own expectations.

By now, I hope my view is clear that one cannot fail to take a position; being silent or immobile or calm are no less influential actions than being aloof or impassioned or attacking or asleep. We cannot refrain from acting; we can only seek to make the impact of our actions available for consideration. An interpretation is a statement of the analyst's agenda. Thus, it carries the influence of the analyst's choice of what is important enough to comment on or trivial enough to ignore. It carries the stamp of the analyst's character, conflicts, and transference to the patient. It is also a disruption and the taking of an unexpected position by the analyst. It must therefore be influential in many ways beyond its lexical content. I believe this is what Gill had in mind when he commented from the floor at a panel (1991) on Eissler's (1953) paper on parameters: "Every interpretation, by definition, is a parameter."

The Analyst's Authority

I would like to turn next to consider some of the influences that must be brought to bear to set the stage for interpretive work. I would frame the question this way: How does the analyst gain the authority to have her perspective taken seriously? The traditional assumption – that the correctness of the interpretation gives the analyst credibility – no longer seems adequate.

We are very much aware that, however reasonable patients may be about seeking treatment, they have powerful motives to turn the treatment into something other than the collaborative search for expanded self-awareness. Sufficiently muted derivatives of sexual and aggressive wishes certainly contribute to our patients' willingness to go along with the program, even if they harbor secret hopes for rewards other than self-knowledge.

Freud's (1912) formulation of the (so-called) "unobjectionable" part of the transference was probably the first formulation of a "therapeutic alliance," which might be thought of as an amalgam of transference-based and "reasonable" attitudes that, at least at a given moment, move the treatment along by investing the analyst with the authority to take the *analyst's* project seriously.

In practice, it is probably impossible to separate transference-based and "reasonable" motives for the patient to grant authority to the analyst, but, for the sake of this explication, I would like to distinguish among (1) the authority the analyst has by virtue of expertise and experience; (2) the authority granted the analyst by virtue of the patient's transference expectations; and (3) the influence of the analyst's manipulations.

The analyst's "legitimate" authority is rarely mentioned as an important influence on the patient, possibly because it seems to go without saying, but perhaps also because it is easily mistaken for authoritarianism, which is anathema to us. Nonetheless, probably every analyst has at one time or another pointed out the paradox in the behavior of the patient who seeks the help of the analyst-as-expert and then refuses her recommendations. We recognize the legitimate authority of our expertise when we encounter patients who challenge it. With other patients, we are more likely to rely on this kind of influence than we are to notice it. It is completely appropriate for the analyst to make recommendations about the frequency or the use of the couch or the "fundamental rule" because she has experience and knowledge about the utility of the procedures. Of course, we do not dictate terms, but we should expect our authoritative (not authoritarian) statements to carry some weight, and we investigate when they do not.

With respect to the authority vested in the analyst by the patient's transference expectations: Many analysts will talk privately about having to "seduce" patients into treatment – though few will commit that to print. Loewald (1971) referred to the "appeal" to the patient to understand unconscious activity as her own: "It is a moral appeal. ... [T]he success of psychoanalytic treatment depends on the patient's aroused propensity to heed this appeal. This is implicit in the therapeutic or working alliance" (p. 95). He says of this appeal, "Undoubtedly there is suggestion at work here" (p. 93).

Martin Stein (1981) emphasized the need to analyze the "unobjectionable positive transference." But that does not imply that we are not using its power as we do so. The exercise of the analyst's transference-based authority does not replace the need to analyze it; in fact, it may be that enacting it is a necessary precondition for its analysis. This is not to suggest that the analyst's use of transference-based authority is contrived or premeditated; rather, it arises spontaneously from the recursive examination of the interaction that makes up the text of the analysis.

This view is at odds with what I think is the more generally held position that suggestion is a contaminant, albeit an inevitable contaminant, of ideal technique. I do not believe it has been demonstrated that patients can be motivated to engage in treatment without the analyst's initially unanalyzed participation in a role in the patient's fantasies. At any rate, it is impossible to avoid such participation and impossible to analyze it until it has taken place. Thus, the suggestive influence of the analyst's transference-based authority is at work, irrespective of the analyst's intentions.

It is something of a paradox that perhaps the most important use to which we put our transference-based authority is to influence the patient to question that authority. In the film *Monty Python's Life of Brian*, a man has been mistaken for the Messiah. When he realizes a crowd is following him, he turns and shouts, "Go away! Think for yourselves!" But he is a prophet in their mind, so they continue to follow, all the while faithfully parroting his words, chanting mindlessly, "Think for yourselves!"[1]

It does seem to be the case that patients manage to learn to think for themselves out of love for (or defiance of) the analyst, although how that happens is a subject that warrants more study. Freud's (1912) understanding was that the "unobjectionable" part of the transference was the vehicle of analytic success: "We take care of the patient's final *independence* by employing *suggestion* in order to get him to accomplish a piece of psychical work which has as its necessary result a permanent improvement in his psychical situation" (p. 106; italics added). Freud apparently did not see it as problematic that we use our transference authority to free the patient from our transference authority, though it may be argued that Freud did not sufficiently distinguish his transference authority from his legitimate authority.

We certainly appeal to the patient's reason when we address the "unobjectionable" transference, or the patient's attempt to ignore the evidence of those of our missteps of which we are aware; but that is not all we do when we interpret. We also display our character, and often the patient is in a better position to make sense of our unconscious motivations than we are. If we seek to keep the influence of our character out of the process by adhering to an elusive ideal of neutrality, we run the risk of rendering that influence off limits to analysis, as Renik (1993b) and others have shown. If, on the other hand, we recognize the inevitability of suggestive influence in any human interaction, we are in a better position to make it available for examination by both patient and analyst. I assume that "suggestion" implies the interaction between the patient's transference-based "suggestibility" and the analyst's transference-colored activity.

This activity may be either in the form of inadvertent "countertransference" enactment or of manipulation, i.e., the analyst's intention to influence the patient by something other than the application of reason to observable facts. Some manipulations are so much a part of analytic technique that we take them for granted. Consider, for example, the very powerful influence we bring to bear by the arrangements we make. The physical ones, e.g., the couch, the soundproofed and comfortable room, the regular appointment times, and so on, are influential in ways with which we are familiar. We also make emotional arrangements in the form of tacit or explicit promises about our behavior and attitudes. We promise an uncommon focus of attention; we promise an unbiased, nonjudgmental attitude; we promise to exercise uncommon restraint; we promise not to seduce, abandon, or retaliate. Of course, we do not deliver on all of these promises; in fact, the promises themselves are powerfully seductive.

Our vocabulary for these aspects of the treatment situation reveals the intent of the manipulation. We refer to the "frame" as if it were a secure boundary, separate from our activity. We refer to the analyst's so-called "neutrality" and "abstinence" as if they were the absence of activity, when in fact they are powerful actions and enticements to the patient to trust and reveal. We talk about a "field" that we try to keep "uncontaminated" by the analyst's activities, when in fact the field is partly an *expression* of the analyst's activities. Even relational analysts who advocate the "technical" use of personal disclosure are making the choice of what to disclose in order to shape the patient's emotional response. Like the doctor who tells the child that the injection will not hurt a bit, we are lying, but it is a useful and influential lie; it is in the patient's best interest, and, in fact, the shot does not hurt as much as the child expected.

I have chosen such deliberately provocative terms as manipulation and lying to emphasize that they are intentionally influential noninterpretive acts. We do try to make the patient feel safe and welcome and accepted. Once the influence of these maneuvers is acknowledged, we are in a position to analyze it. But if we insist that we are not acting when, for example, we listen attentively, we will limit and distort our understanding of the patient's experience.

Looking back with the patient, we can (and should) face squarely the fact that we *did* use the power of our office, we *did* (however inadvertently) play the role the patient perceived, and we *did* serve our own motives as well as the patient's; we could not have done otherwise. And we expect that, looking back, the patient will come to appreciate the complexity of human motives, including her own, in a richer and more understanding way.

Note

1 In Woody Allen's film *Broadway Danny Rose*, there is a parrot that sings "I Gotta Be Me" (Levenson, 1991).

References

Eissler, K.R. (1953). The effect of the structure of the ego on psychoanalytic technique. *Journal of the American Psychoanalytic Association, 1*, 104–43.

Freud, S. (1912). The dynamics of transference. SE *12*, 97–108.

Gill, M.M. (1982). *Analysis of transference, Vol. 1: Theory and technique.* International Universities Press.

Gill, M.M. (1991). Indirect suggestion: A response to Oremland's "Interpretation and interaction." In J.D. Oremland (Ed.), *Interpretation and interaction: Psychoanalysis or psychotherapy?* (pp. 137–64). Analytic Press.

Glover, E. (1931). The therapeutic effect of inexact interpretation: A contribution to the theory of suggestion. *The International Journal of Psychoanalysis, 12*, 397–411.

Laing, R.D. (1965). *The divided self.* Penguin.

Levenson, E.A. (1991). *The purloined self. Interpersonal perspectives in psychoanalysis.* William Alanson White Institute.

Loewald, H.W. (1971). *Papers on psychoanalysis.* Yale University Press (1980).

Panel (1991). Classics revisited: Eissler's "The effect of the structure of the ego on psychoanalytic technique." L. Friedman, chair. Presented at the Fall Meeting of the American Psychoanalytic Association, New York.

Poland, W.S. (1975). Tact as a psychoanalytic function. *The International Journal of Psychoanalysis, 56*, 155–62.

Renik, O. (1993a). Countertransference enactment and the psychoanalytic process. In M. J. Horowitz, O. F. Kernberg, & E. M. Weinshel (Eds.), *Psychic structure and psychic change: Essays in honor of Robert S. Wallerstein, M.D.* (pp. 135–58). International Universities Press.

Renik, O. (1993b). Analytic interaction: Conceptualizing technique in light of the analyst's irreducible subjectivity. *The Psychoanalytic Quarterly, 62*, 553–71.

Stein, M.H. (1981). The unobjectionable part of the transference. *Journal of the American Psychoanalytic Association, 29*(4), 869–92.

Chapter 12

What the Analyst Does Not Hear

At an American Psychoanalytic Association workshop on analytic listening, Arnold Goldberg (Workshop, 1995) posed a key question to one of the presenters: How do you know when you are wrong? I would like to offer some musings on that question, then raise a subsidiary question: Can we incorporate the fact that we are wrong much (if not most) of the time into our thinking about analytic work? To put the question somewhat differently: How can we best understand the role of what we do not hear in the analytic process as we listen to our patients and ourselves? Let me say at the outset that I have no satisfactory answer; my ambition for this contribution is limited to bringing the question into sharper relief.

I would like to begin the discussion with a brief clinical illustration to highlight the difficulty of accounting for what we do not hear.

Ms. F

A woman writer came to analysis because of a series of unsatisfying romantic involvements with men. Despite being sought after by many men, and despite many satisfying casual friendships with bright and talented people, she harbored the conviction that she could not be too choosy in her romantic life. Repeatedly she seemed to find herself with men with whom she felt little or no connection, emotionally or intellectually.

Ms. F was the only child of an artist and critic father and a mother of limited education and ambition. As her father became more celebrated, her mother became increasingly isolated and withdrawn. Finally, as Ms. F was entering adolescence, her parents split up. She was devoted to her mother, whom she felt had been wronged by her father, but it gradually emerged that she also felt convinced that she had been a more suitable companion to her father than her mother had been. She shared his interests in a way the mother was unable to do, and, as might be expected, she struggled with a sense of responsibility for the divorce.

Much of the early work centered around the ways in which Ms. F sold herself short, and how that seemed to calm certain anxieties. She had chosen me

DOI: 10.4324/9781003360391-15

over many better-known analysts because she had never heard of me; she did not feel it right for her to take one of the "stars" from someone else. As the work progressed, she became less anxious, and freer in her enjoyment of the company of men. Her opinion of me improved as well; it soon became clear that she found our interaction stimulating and enjoyable.

Well into the analysis, Ms. F complained about an insensitive remark made by the man she was dating at the time. She then shrugged it off as not typical of him. I heard her readiness to dismiss her complaint as another example of selling herself short, and I commented that she seemed to be saying she did not deserve better. This remark was met with a brief but noticeable silence, after which the patient made it clear that I was mistaken. I had not heard that she was serious about the man she was seeing, whom she found exciting and admirable.

She then said, "You know, you've been making that same interpretation for a long time. I get the feeling that you think the only person good enough for me is you." She was quick to add that she guessed it was "just wishful thinking" on her part. We were familiar with some versions of the wishes in question, which had been explored profitably in the past, and to which she now returned.

After some time, I commented on her use of the word "just," and I suggested that she was more comfortable seeing the issue as purely her doing than she was considering the implications of what she saw in me. She realized that was so. She found it unsettling. It was flattering, exciting, but I was not supposed to be interested in her that way. It also felt like a burden. She wanted to get on with her life, not spend it in analysis. I said she seemed to be fighting the feeling that she had to accommodate me by not getting on with her life.

As Ms. F thought about that over the next several sessions, a variety of issues opened up. She experienced the dilemma of being caught between two people she loved, and she felt that she was being asked to choose, as she had felt about the divorce. She reviewed this experience of me alternately as my needing her to take care of me and as my being excited by her. The former brought up thoughts of her concerns for her mother at the time of the divorce. The latter reminded her of an incident in which she had noticed that her father was sexually aroused in her presence.

At first Ms. F had condemned her father for being aroused. Subsequently, she became aware of a sense of guilt for her presumed role in the incident. She could now recall that she had also felt excited at the discovery that she was capable of arousing him, and she realized that nothing untoward had happened. As she turned back to her experience with me, she began to consider the possibility that she and I could enjoy a mutual excitement that did not constitute a claim on her or stop her from loving someone else.

I would like to review this example in terms of how I listened, and what I did and did not hear, in several stages. What I heard, first, was that Ms. F was selling herself short with her choice of men in order to lessen her anxiety about being capable of attracting a more suitable man. I had not heard that she was happy and excited about the new man she was seeing. I will comment later on how I heard her response to my interpretation and how it affected my subsequent listening, but first I will describe some possible readings of the events.

From one perspective, the patient responded to my remark by hearing it as evidence for the transference fantasy that I wanted to keep her for myself. I invited her to elaborate, and two transference configurations emerged, corresponding to her perceptions of her mother and father, that I was competing with other men for her. I believe this is a reasonable description, as far as it goes. It conveys some important movement in the analytic work. From one listening perspective, it might be the end of the description: The patient construed the analyst's meaning in accordance with her preformed transference expectations, which she then elaborated.

From this standpoint, the analyst's motives are irrelevant, and it is taken for granted that his actions are in the service of the analysis – i.e., all the analyst did was interpret; the interpretation could be inaccurate, ill-timed, or incomplete, but anything the patient experiences other than the analyst's analytic intent is so powerfully determined by the patient's transference that one can safely treat the outcome as the patient's creation.

Another reading of the events might add another dimension – namely, that my countertransference contributed to what I heard and how I listened. According to this view, we might consider the "contamination of the field" by the intrusion of the analyst's unconscious process: My own unconscious motives compromised what I heard and how I listened *in this instance*. This view presumes that there are times when the analyst's unconscious motives do *not* contribute in an important way to the patient's experience.

If that was how I listened to myself listening, I could consider my intervention to be a mistake and relegate its understanding to my self-analysis. The significance for the analysis of the patient would be limited to attention to the impact of my mistake, advantageous or otherwise. Since (from this perspective) it was a departure from an analytic stance, it is part of the analysis only as a breach. In other words, it need not be incorporated into a theory of technique.

An alternative formulation taking "countertransference" considerations into account would look to my experience as information about the patient's activity, for example via projective identification. Here let me add something of my actual experience to the report. When the patient told me she heard me as saying the only person good enough for her was I, my immediate (and disturbing) reaction was to see that there was some truth in what she was saying. I had been feeling that "someday" she would be ready to leave analysis, but I realized that I so enjoyed her that I was reluctant to think that "someday" would actually come.

From the perspective of countertransference as information about the patient, I could have listened to my reaction as one stimulated by her projected wishes. It was not a great leap to recognize that the view of me as wanting to keep her, or the view of her father as being aroused by her, or the view of her mother as being nothing without her, all had wishful elements; she subsequently confirmed as much.

This view makes the same epistemological assumptions as the first description, in which the patient's preformed transferences eclipse any other concern. Both construe the analyst's listening as a primarily passive, receptive process. Countertransference, in this usage, is a reaction to transference.[1]

The striking feature of all these views is the implication that the rules governing the analyst's psychology are different from those governing the patient's. We do not expect our patients' perceptions to be free of unconscious determinants; indeed, we insist that this is never so. But certain listening perspectives implicitly depend on the implausible assumption that the analyst can suspend her unconscious motives in analytic listening. This is true whether we see ourselves as detached, objective, mirrorlike observers (Freud, 1912) or as empathic receivers of the patient's projected experience (Ogden, 1979).

I would like to return to the example to try to take the fact of the analyst's psychology into account in two ways: first, to show how I actually listened in the clinical moment (which I think will be consistent with a view that is reflected in much of the current literature); and second, to begin to address the problem of how to approach what we do not hear as part of the process.

When my patient responded to my interpretation, she made her own interpretation of one unconscious meaning of my actions. My reaction confirmed (at least to my satisfaction) that she was onto something, which I understood as far as I have described above. Although I was not very comfortable with what she said, I did not suggest that her perception was mistaken. Moreover, at the time I felt that, by virtue of her external perspective, she had inferred one of my unconscious motives about which I knew very little.

This experience affected my subsequent listening in many ways, two of which I would like to highlight. First, it brought to the forefront of my attention what I accept in principle but do not always bear in mind: that my own unconscious activity was playing a role in the interaction. Second, it forced me to realize that I was operating on a theory about the patient that needed reconsideration. Ms. F had told me I was wrong. That did not mean she was right, but it did remind me not to assume that I was right.

By addressing the patient's effort to dismiss her perception of me as "*just* wishful thinking," I tried to keep the subject on the table between us. At the time I was not sure of the extent of my contribution, but I tried to be sure that it was available for our discussion by addressing her effort to disavow it, and by trying to avoid any suggestion that would covertly challenge her perception. I did not confirm its accuracy; it was, after all, her own version of something I actually did, and so it was neither strictly accurate, nor strictly a distortion. Furthermore, she had considered only one of my motives; there were others of which I was aware, and doubtless still others of which I was not. But neither did I refer to her interpretation of my actions as her "fantasy" or even as her "wish" – which I think would have implied that I would have preferred that we ignore what I had done to stir it up.

I believe that proceeding this way had a useful impact, which was to help the patient see that this very human exchange of feelings did not necessarily compromise our work or her life choices (it was useful to me for the same reason, although that was not what she was paying me for). In the larger scheme of things, it was useful because it confronted the patient with the fact that my unconscious activity was a part of the interaction for which we could both listen. Patients often seek to disavow or discredit their perceptions of the analyst, and it is all too tempting for the analyst to let that happen.

In describing the vignette as I just did, I believe it will be familiar to readers as representative of a particular "relational" trend in the analytic literature, even among so-called "classical" analysts. Many analysts have become increasingly interested in their own unconscious contribution to the process. Jacobs (1986), for example, has contributed many elegant instances of his involvement in subtle unconscious enactments. In each case he described how his own self-scrutiny undid an impasse and ultimately moved the work forward. Gill (1982) has emphasized the connection of all transference to the actual analytic situation. Boesky (1990) has offered a view of the process that emphasizes a reconceptualization of many resistances as a joint creation. Renik (2007), among many others, has taken up the intersubjective nature of the analytic encounter. Hoffman (1983) has written about the patient as interpreter of the analyst's experience.

Our literature has been enriched by many such contributions, of which this is only a tiny sampling. I share with most of those authors the impression that the analytic process consists of the recursive study of complex interactions, of which the analyst is co-author, with the goal of helping the patient toward useful self-awareness. My way of thinking about what I did owes much to the above contributors, although I am slightly more uneasy than some of my colleagues about making technical recommendations, for reasons I will explain in due course.

The best of these contributions is built on clinical material that shows how the analyst – by listening to the patient, by listening to the patient listening to the analyst, and by listening to herself listening to the patient – can bring much that was previously unnoticed into the discussion. In my example, my patient's comment made me listen to how I had been listening, and it provided the opportunity for me to enlist her participation in noticing how she listened to me. In many of the cases in the literature, we come away with a respect, sometimes bordering on awe, for what the analyst is eventually able to hear. But there is an implication in all of these writings, and one that is certainly not what the various authors intended: that by the end of the vignette, the situation will have been understood.

These vignettes are publishable because they are exemplary moments of understanding. But most of the analysis takes place in long stretches between those moments when we feel we understand. Furthermore, even at those moments, what we do not know far outweighs what we know. In this sense, even the best of the analytic literature does not reflect the actual experience of analytic work. That is, of course, an artifact of writing: We write about what we know and not about what we do not know. My example is, after all, an example of what I finally came to hear; it does not, and could not, deal explicitly with what I never heard.

We spend far more of our time mired in uncertainty than otherwise. In my experience at least, the state in which I spend the most analytic time is one of feeling that *something* is going on but I do not know what it is, other than to notice some almost ineffable tension between my patient and me. Periodically, we learn something, but never everything, about it. Even those moments of apparent epiphany usually prove in retrospect to be something more than what I thought had been happening. It is often the case that what we feel sure of turns out to be a misleading partial truth. Gradually, our understanding comes into clearer resolution, and we have a sense of the work moving forward; but, at any given moment, what we do not understand far outweighs what we do understand.

It should be clear by now how complex and profound a question Goldberg posed when he asked how we know when we are wrong. Often we do not know. It is tempting to quip that the one time we are sure to be wrong is when we feel certain we are right. The patient's agreement with our ideas is no guarantee of correctness; we often discover collusions and compliance, although I suspect that, in every analysis, they remain undetected far more often than not.

In my clinical example, it was easy to suspect that I might have been wrong. The patient told me so, and she told me her ideas about why I was wrong. Those situations may be challenging, but they are not the main difficulty. In the instance cited, I did not have to speculate about the silent operation of my unconscious processes, because my patient slapped me in the face with them. One inference I draw from the clinical example is that, for every instance in which a patient is able to alert me to the possibility that I might be wrong, there must be countless examples in which I never notice I am wrong.

So the question arises: How do we take our struggling in the dark into account in our thinking about analytic technique? Our published clinical vignettes almost always show us reaching a satisfying understanding, even if it follows a protracted struggle. But this skews our picture of the analytic process toward an idealization and may make us embarrassed by the confusion, tension, and relative ignorance that is (or, in my view, should be!) our day-to-day state.

Clinical vignettes do not easily demonstrate the more typically muddy analytic situation. Perhaps it would be useful to imagine an "anti-vignette" that would encompass the volume of clinical material that does not get reported because we never understand it, or never even notice that there is anything to understand. For example, an "anti-vignette" true to analytic experience would consist of all that I do not remember or do not notice about what went on in each hour of a given day. Here is what I could say about my participation in those unrecorded moments: I know that I did something with each patient, motivated by something I did not understand, which was in some measure a response to the patient (and therefore includes some contribution on her part), and which was also an expression of my own psychology. I do not know my unconscious motives for what I did; I do not know how to separate my contribution from the patient's; I do not know what will turn out to be important to the patient and what will not. And I do not know if I will ever find out.

I certainly expect that I will learn a great deal about *some* of the overlooked interactions as clinical events bring them to my mind or to the patient's mind. So some of my ignorance is an artifact of my choice to restrict my example to one day. But I suspect that much, if not most, of what goes on in my office will remain undiscovered. That is a limitation of the clinical art that we live with. When circumstances bring something previously unconscious to awareness, we have a clinical vignette; when they do not, we do not. We do not know what we do not know; what is unconscious is unconscious, and that applies to the analyst as well as to the patient.

What implications does this fact have for clinical work? It means, among other things, that we need to allow that the patient is often in a better position to notice the manifestations of the analyst's unconscious processes than the analyst is (Hoffman, 1983). The analyst has a valuable and different perspective on the patient largely (though not exclusively) because it is a view from the outside; the same may be said of the patient's perspective on the analyst. Neither view is free of subjective bias (that is, of transference); neither party can ever be certain.

These facts lead me to number myself among those who view the analytic task as a collaborative effort to understand the interpersonal events of analysis as they happen, with neither party having special access to truth. The goal of such a view is to try to help the patient maximize not only the capacity to observe herself but also the capacity to observe the analyst in order to make optimal use of the analyst in the service of helpful self-awareness.

It is not obvious how that goal is to be achieved, and I have only the most tentative and general suggestions to make as to how to think about it. Many authors have offered ways to move in that direction, but each has its associated pitfalls. For example, Hoffman's (1983) advocacy of willful self-disclosure is designed to facilitate collaborative work, including giving the patient the opportunity to interpret the analyst's experience, but Hoffman (1994) also suggests the need to leave undisturbed certain of the patient's magical illusions about the analyst. Thus, the analyst chooses to self-disclose at some times and not at others. If this is a technical problem, what principle can we teach our students to guide the choice?

In any case, the least the analyst can do is strive not to make the collaborative task of the patient and the analyst observing each other and themselves together any harder than it need be. A particular maneuver such as willful self-disclosure may not succeed as a universal prescription for making the analyst's unconscious activity available to the participants in the analysis, but, as we have seen, certain *attitudes* can serve as obstacles to the full accounting of the analyst's contribution.

The analyst's *conviction* that she is merely an observer will certainly convey to the patient the analyst's wish that the two of them need not take the patient's perceptions of the analyst seriously. Whether the patient tacitly agrees, or subtly complies to protect the analyst, the outcome is that an important segment of the patient's experience is summarily excluded from analytic consideration. The same reasoning applies to the analyst who has the conviction that everything she feels in the hour has been "put into" her by the patient. In fact, the same may be said of the analyst who insists on a more "egalitarian" stance – if, for example, the analyst is unwilling to consider the possibility that the patient's perception of the analyst as authoritarian might have some basis in the analyst's behavior.

Renik (1995) has made many of these same observations. At the same time that he warns against the analyst cultivating unearned authority by adhering to a counterproductive ideal of anonymity (p. 494), he also points out that any doctrine, no matter how humble or egalitarian in theory, can be used in the service of authoritarian or other anti-analytic goals (p. 484). He argues for the need for an "ethic of candor" (p. 494).

This brings me to my uneasiness about technical recommendations. Although I am in substantial agreement with what Renik has to say, I am not sure that the matter properly falls under the rubric of technique at all. When he refers to analysts using an ideal of anonymity to cultivate unearned authority, I believe that the main problem he is identifying is that analysts may use their theories of technique to rationalize aspects of their character. And, as he suggests, no theoretical position is immune from that use. When he then recommends an *ethic* of candor, he is recommending not a technical device, but an *attitude* – again, one that (I believe) cuts across particular technical approaches.

In the discussion of my clinical example, I tried to show how analysts of various persuasions might have listened to the patient and what they would have heard, in accordance with their theoretical ideas. But I suspect that both our way of listening and our preference for theories are primarily consequences of our way of seeing ourselves. It may be true that theory shapes technique,[2] but, to a far greater extent, character shapes theoretical preference.

Of course, that applies to me as well, and to my emphasis in this chapter on aspects of the clinical situation that I think we might be inclined to neglect. But no technical approach has a monopoly on candor or honesty or empathy; nor, as Renik suggested, is any technical approach a guarantee against defensive or exploitative use. I believe that we are inclined to confuse our character traits (for example, activity or passivity) with our technique because we are stuck with our character traits. But I will leave the further elaboration of this position for the next chapter.

In a sense, the villain in the piece is the analyst's posture of certainty — a character trait, not a technical device. The analyst's realization of the limits of knowledge, of both herself and of the patient, helps set a collaborative tone in the work and makes it possible to address the patient's idealization of the analyst as omniscient. On the other hand, if we subscribe to a view of ourselves that says we *should always* know, or to a position that says we can translate anything we feel into a *fact* about the patient, we are in danger of colluding with the patient's passivity and idealization of the analyst and of discouraging the patient from questioning the analyst's authority in favor of her own.

The analyst's unconscious personal (or professional) myths are no less tenacious than the patient's. We know it is a valuable practice to attempt an ongoing "self-analysis" in the course of our work; but, beyond that, we need to give full weight to the fact that we are governed by unconscious forces just as our patients are. And we need to modify our attitudes to take that into account. At a minimum, that means not only being aware of the limits of our understanding of ourselves with our patients but also insisting that our patients do not avoid awareness of those limits. Our interpretations are hypotheses, filtered through our own perceptions; if our patients treat them as other than our personal impressions, we must explore their efforts to hear them the way they do.

These observations imply the endless nature of the quest to understand the patient and the limits of the *analyst's* capacity to provide such understanding. This shifts more of the responsibility for the ongoing work onto the patient. Analytic listening is still listening *for* the patient, but it must be listening *to* *both* parties in the interaction, and it must become listening *by both* parties. This means that, somehow, the patient's participation as a listener to both parties must be actively sought, and the patient's efforts to evade that responsibility must be actively confronted. Analytic listening is not something the analyst does to the patient. No matter how enlightened a listener, the analyst will hear only what she can hear in accordance with her own unconscious motives. Therefore, there must be two listeners attending to two actors striving toward a shared perspective about the patient. And, as I suggested, I am more inclined to think of this effort as establishing an attitude rather than as exercising a technique.

How do we know when we are wrong? Ultimately, we do not know. Perhaps, after all, it is the wrong question. A more practical question may be in order: How do we know if we are helping the patient with the problems that brought her into the office? The approach of analysis is to study the interaction in order to expand the patient's capacity to feel and to reflect. We judge that we are on the right track by looking for signs of that expansion: Is the patient taking more ownership of her difficulties? Are the people the patient describes becoming more nuanced and complex? Are the patient's goals evolving, or are they retaining a magical character?

Hour by hour we try to prevent the foreclosure of any thought or feeling, but that runs counter to human nature, ours and the patient's. We have no guarantee against failure. Our best chance of success is to enlist the patient as a collaborator in the listening task as fully as possible.

Notes

1   Note how often we refer to "countertransference" and how rarely we refer to the analyst's transference to the patient (Bird, 1972; McLaughlin, 1981; see also Part III).
2   It would probably be more correct to say that theory shapes theory of technique.

References

Bird, B. (1972). Notes on transference: Universal phenomenon and hardest part of analysis. *Journal of the American Psychoanalytic Association, 20*(2), 267–301.

Boesky, D. (1990). The psychoanalytic process and its components. *The Psychoanalytic Quarterly, 59*(4), 550–84.

Freud, S. (1912). Recommendations to physicians practising psycho-analysis. SE *12*, 109–20.

Gill, M.M. (1982). *Analysis of transference. Vol. 1. Theory and technique.* International Universities Press.

Hoffman, I.Z. (1983). The patient as interpreter of the analyst's experience. *Contemporary Psychoanalysis, 19*(3), 389–422.

Hoffman, I.Z. (1994). Dialectical thinking and therapeutic action in the psychoanalytic process. *The Psychoanalytic Quarterly, 63*(2), 187–218.

Jacobs, T.J. (1986). On countertransference enactments. *Journal of the American Psychoanalytic Association, 34*(2), 289–307.

McLaughlin, J.T. (1981). Transference, psychic reality, and countertransference. *The Psychoanalytic Quarterly, 50*(4), 639–64.

Ogden, T.H. (1979). On projective identification. *The International Journal of Psychoanalysis, 60*(3), 357–73.

Renik, O. (1995). The ideal of the anonymous analyst and the problem of self-disclosure. *The Psychoanalytic Quarterly, 64*(3), 466–95.

Renik, O. (2007). Intersubjectivity, therapeutic action, and analytic technique. *The Psychoanalytic Quarterly*, 76(Suppl.), 1547–62.

Smith, H.F. (1995). Analytic listening and the experience of surprise. *The International Journal of Psychoanalysis*, 76(1), 67–78.

Workshop (1995). How does the analyst listen? What does the analyst hear? Sponsored by the American Psychoanalytic Association, San Francisco.

Chapter 13

Analytic Technique

A Reconsideration of the Concept

As our notions of the analytic process have evolved, our ideas of what constitutes proper analytic technique have become more and more hotly contested. For example, principles of neutrality and abstinence, once considered basic to technique, have been attacked, defended, and redefined. The analyst is no longer a "blank slate" for the patient's projections – what, if anything, does that mean for technique? If the analyst's subjectivity is "irreducible," as Renik (1993a) argued, what, if anything, does that say about how we proceed? How much of ourselves should we disclose willfully, and how do we make those decisions?

In a paper that has become a neglected classic, Lipton (1977) made three cogent observations about the concept of technique. First, he pointed out that sometime between Freud's time and his own, the usage of the term "technique" changed from a description of the analyst's *purpose* to a description of her *actions*, considered independent of the particular clinical situation. Second, he suggested that many of the analyst's actions fall outside the realm of technique. Third, he questioned whether it made sense to conceptualize technique without including the variable of the personality of the analyst (Lipton, 1977, p. 264). More recently, Gorman (2008), also citing Lipton, proposed a shift of attention from the analyst's technique to her analytic attitude and intention.

Consideration of these and similar challenging questions have moved our field forward in important ways. In this chapter I would like to elaborate on some of Lipton's ideas and suggest that we have reached the time in our discourse to consider an even more basic question about analytic technique: What does it mean to conceive of a "technique" for analysis at all?

At some point in training, most of us have had the opportunity to listen to two acknowledged masters dispute the analytic work of one of them. It has often been the case that each participant insisted more or less (usually less) politely that what she was doing was analysis, and what the other was doing was not. Yet in my experience I often found that, despite these dramatic differences, I retained the sense that each was a superb analyst; when I had occasion to seek a referral for a family member, I was delighted if either was available.

DOI: 10.4324/9781003360391-16

This led me to reconsider the question of what makes a good analyst in a somewhat different light. I began with the assumption that, to understand what made them both good analysts, I had to look for what they had in common, something that neither included in her theory of technique. In what follows I suggest that those common attributes exist, that they are not typically considered matters of technique at all, and that one of those attributes is an attitude we might consider to be the *opposite* of technique.

I would like to try to capture something of the experience I had in listening to two accomplished analysts debate. I have overdrawn the participants for effect, but I expect that they will be recognizable as types. I call them Dr. A (for "active") and Dr. P (for "passive"). Dr. A's work was striking for the "mix it up" quality of her interactions with patients. She was very active, as measured by how much she spoke in her hours; she pushed the patient to consider ideas; and she pursued any hint that the patient was deferring to the analyst's authority. She insisted that the patient take responsibility for himself, even as they were discussing his difficulties doing so. She was relentless.

Dr. A was free with her opinions and emphatic in her presentation of them. When she thought the patient was going to do something that was not in his best interest, she would challenge the patient forcefully. When a patient would complain that she was pushing him, she would pursue the patient's sense that he had to agree with the analyst. In situations in which she felt the patient was not willing to do the work, she was ready to suggest that, unless the patient could be more forthcoming, they should stop the analysis. She tended to keep her eye on the goal of symptom relief and sought to avoid distractions. Her analyses tended to be somewhat shorter than the national average. When I listened to her work, I pictured her as a warrior engaged in a battle, more interested in obtaining the objective than in exploring the terrain.

By contrast, Dr. P's work was striking for the "unflappable" quality of his interactions with patients. He was very calm and even in his tone. He spoke much less than Dr. A. He rarely expressed an opinion. When a patient faced a life decision, he insisted that he was not in a position to judge, although he was not hesitant to point out that the patient herself had betrayed an opinion she was not seeing. He would never unilaterally suggest interrupting or ending a treatment, and he would never voice an opinion about a patient's wish to stop, beyond trying to analyze the meaning of the wish as an association to other material in the hour. He tended to emphasize the richness of human experience and saw the process as one of stopping to smell the analytic roses rather than trying to get to the end. His analyses tended to be somewhat longer than the national average. When I listened to his work, I pictured him as a reader engrossed in a novel, more interested in the development and the characters than in the denouement.

Each of these analysts taught an approach to analysis that was consistent with the way they worked. Dr. A called herself an intersubjectivist and subscribed to Renik's (1993b) view of the analytic process as a series of mutual emotional entanglements that were understood after the fact. Dr. P called himself a contemporary conflict theorist and talked about the analytic process as the careful reading and communicating to the patient of the patient's anxieties, the unconscious fantasies that stimulated them, and the strategies the patient used to manage them.

Each of these analysts understood the goal of analysis as helping the patient obtain useful self-awareness. They differed in their thinking about how best to achieve that goal. Dr. A pointed out that "transference" is a ubiquitous phenomenon in the analyst as well as in the patient; she reasoned that the analyst has no privileged psychological position, and therefore the task of analysis was to engage the patient as an active partner in a search for personal truth, insisting that the patient face his observation of the analyst's psychology as well as his own in order to discover something about himself. She insisted that the analyst does not and cannot know the patient's truth, and that must be made explicit. Dr. P insisted that, although transference is ubiquitous, the analyst does not have a personal stake in the patient's struggles, and he is therefore less subject to the pressures that lead to unrealistic distortions. He argued that it was the patient's conflicts that drove the analysis, and the analyst was less compromised by them because they were not his own. Also, by virtue of having been analyzed himself, the analyst was more aware of the areas in which his own distortions are likely to come into play.

Dr. A sees Dr. P's efforts toward neutrality as a harmful myth that leads to a collusion between patient and analyst to idealize the analyst and rule the analyst's psychology out of bounds for discussion. Dr. P concedes that neutrality is never achieved, but he believes that it can be approximated to the point that it is a useful effort. He sees Dr. A's activity as preempting the patient's self-expression and turning the analytic effort into the analysis of the analyst. Reading between the lines, it is clear that each sees *the other's* approach as an expression of her own problems or character structure.

I think the preceding descriptions, admittedly caricatured, will not be unfamiliar to most analysts. They represent two positions in an ongoing debate over the nature of the analytic process and the implications for technique. But I began by saying that these are two superb analysts; that opinion is shared by many who know them both, despite the fact that most of us come down strongly on one side or the other of the debate. What makes them superb analysts?

To begin with, everyone who listens to either of them present cases hears something more than their theories. Each of these analysts clearly cares about their patients. Each has a noticeable investment in helping patients learn about themselves. More specifically, each *conveys* a sense that she is working to understand, and help the patient understand, the nature of the patient's dilemmas. Each conveys a respect for the patient and her situation, even if each sees a different way to be helpful. Although each teaches a technique for analysis, listeners to their actual work do not hear "techniques"; they hear two different people trying to find their way with their patients.

How is it that we can have such strong feelings about the "right" way to analyze, yet (when there is something personal at stake, such as the well-being of a relative) we still recognize good analysis in the rival camp? I think the question of what constitutes a good analyst is a bit like the question of what makes a good parent: We may argue for or against permissiveness or limit-setting or discipline or fostering autonomy, but we also know there is a wide range of good parenting, and — more to the point — one does not exactly *decide* what kind of parent to be.

Does one decide what kind of analyst to be? In my view, only superficially. I think that when Dr. A and Dr. P attribute *each other's* approaches to vicissitudes of character, they are both right. The important differences between Dr. A and Dr. P are characterological, and their theories are shaped by rationalizations of the very adaptive and creative expressions of their respective characters. Dr. A is impatient, fighting for the patient's well-being, unwilling to back off; Dr. P is content, allowing the patient to find her own way, unwilling to impose. We might surmise that Dr. A is not comfortable with her passive wishes and Dr. P is not comfortable with his aggressive wishes. Curiously, each finds a way to emphasize the autonomy of the patient: Dr. A demands it by challenging attempts at its abrogation, and Dr. P encourages it by refraining from challenging its unavoidable expression.

I have suggested some of the attributes these two excellent analysts have in common: a sense of a goal — to relieve suffering via the expansion of understanding; a willingness to put that goal ahead of selfish concerns; and a sincere interest in, and respect for, the plight of the patient. There is certainly an implicit theory in the idea of the utility of self-understanding, but it does not dictate how one achieves that goal — that is, it is not itself a theory of technique. The other traits mentioned so far are human qualities that probably fall under the heading of common decency and would not (and, as Lipton pointed out, should not) be considered techniques. It is true that one school of thought talks about empathy as if it were a technical device, but I see that as precisely the kind of confusion I am trying to address. One does not *decide* to apply one's empathy in one clinical situation and withhold it in another; in a given moment, one either is or is not listening empathically.

The Functions of Technique: Rules, Principles, and Attitudes

So far I may have conveyed some sense of the attributes that go into making a good analyst (of any theoretical stripe), which do not fall under the rubric of technique. Having said something of what I think technique is not, I would like to say something about what I think it is. What is meant by analytic technique? I would like to distinguish three concepts, in order of increasing level of abstraction: rules, principles, and attitudes.

Early in training, most of us learned certain rules of procedure that we accepted gratefully as beacons in the analytic darkness. We were taught to start and end on time – even though we might not have been too clear as to why, for most of us it was at least consonant with our intuition that it was a good thing to be consistent and dependable. We were taught to refrain from volunteering personal information, or maybe not to answer questions. We were taught to be tactful and to be honest, but to be careful not to be too friendly (seductive) or judgmental (aggressive). As we gained more experience, we began to see principles behind the rules; we were trying not to contaminate the field, to leave room for the patient to experience and elaborate fantasies, untainted (so we thought) by the analyst's input. We eschewed influencing the patient in any way beyond showing her the facts about her actions – that is, via interpretation. We sought to avoid suggestion as not only unanalytic but anti-analytic, since it played into a myth of the analyst, rather than the patient, as the one who knows what is good for the patient.

We also began to notice that the stories told about our most revered teachers were almost invariably about departures from these rules of technique. In fact, the more we heard of how the acknowledged masters in the field worked, the more it became apparent that they felt free (relative to us aspirants) to ignore the rules we were trying to follow. Were they governed by different principles? Where did their governing principles come from?

Later on, we may have learned new principles of technique that seem to turn those early departures from the rules into new rules – for example, in favor of willful self-disclosure. The beginning analyst is always grateful for rules because the beginning analyst finds the tension and the confusion of possibilities in the analytic situation overwhelming. Rules help us get oriented, so we can at least get started in our work and not feel paralyzed. The difficulty is that the beginner expects that in the future *there will be no more tension.* She is not in a position to realize the truth about analysis that, as Friedman (1988) pointed out, tension is inherent in the analytic encounter (pp. 5–13). And with the security of a technical tool in hand, the analyst may persist in feeling that tension or confusion in the analytic hour is a sign that something is wrong.

The first function of technique, or of a theory of technique, is to help us keep calm in a situation that is inherently tense. It works, in the sense that it alleviates the analyst's discomfort (Friedman, 1988, pp. 14–43). When we need to find a port in an analytic storm, we turn to technique. But we often admire analysts who depart from technique. They do so not because they are calm and self-assured, but because they have accepted the fact that they will be tense and confused much of the time. And we probably sense the fact that anything that is *recognizable* as "technique" smacks of cookbooks, formulas, or other inauthentic reductions of the clinical moment to something impersonal. That is why I suggested that an attribute shared by good analysts is the *opposite* of "technique": It is a unique responsiveness to the patient, to a situation that has never happened before.

A technical rule is something that guides us in *generic* situations; it has broad applicability. "Do not answer a patient's direct question" guides the raw beginner, rightly or wrongly; with more experience it becomes "do not answer without getting associations first." With still more experience we may qualify the rule further, as the underlying *principle* of looking for motivation begins to make more sense. But then the principle itself gets qualified: In some clinical moments some other task may seem more immediately important than looking for motivation.

The more experience we get, the more exceptions there are to technical rules, and even to technical principles. Hoffman (1994) noted that a growing literature about the feeling of clinicians needing to "throw away the book" is ironically becoming the new "book" that still needs to be thrown away. What is left after we throw away the book?

Lipton would argue that the "book" did not exist in Freud's day; his discussion of Freud's having fed the Rat Man a meal, and how he subsequently analyzed the meanings of that event, exemplified how Freud's civility was not a "technical" matter, and that Freud's technique was to do whatever furthered understanding. Lipton pointed out that technique before the "modern" (ca. 1950) era was a matter of the analyst's intentions, not her actions. I would add that it is a matter of *attitude* that determines how a given analyst acts in a given clinical situation. As I hope I illustrated with Drs. A and P, analytic intentions can be pursued with different attitudes, in accordance with the analyst's character.

Warren Poland (2002) described technique as attitude actualized (p. 807); we may add that a given analyst's technique is character rationalized. The present-day definition of analytic technique in terms of the analyst's behavior is a definition on the same order of abstraction as rules. When we shift our thinking to principles, and attend to the role of the individual analyst's attitude in following those principles, we answer Lipton's objection to excluding the analyst's personality from our theorizing about technique.

Once again I would go a step further and say that the concept of technique is itself misleading. The word itself implies transferability from one analyst to another, the way any surgeon can teach any intern how to do a mattress suture. When we do not recognize the contribution of character to technique, we may confuse character traits, which are personal to the individual, with "technique" (hereinafter to be read as if placed in quotation marks), which purports to be generic. In other words, we may try to teach others to analyze in accordance with our character traits rather than in accordance with their own.

The obvious fact that the analyst's character shapes what she will hear and what she will feel with the patient has huge implications for how we think about our work and how we teach. A theory of technique cast in terms of the analyst's *behavior* is an effort to make the analyst's character disappear. If it did so, we could teach analysis by teaching technique. But it does not work that way. A good analyst does not try to be someone else; she tries to use her strengths, receptivity, and (as I argued in the last chapter) tolerance of ignorance to good advantage.

The difficulty is that we have not yet incorporated this fact into our thinking about technique, so we continue to try to rationalize our individual traits into theories of technique, then see them as competing with the theories that rationalize the actions of different kinds of characters. Worse, we may be trying to teach our character as if we were teaching "preferred" technique.

Our work has been enriched in recent years by increasing attention to the "countertransference" as a source of information about the patient and the interaction. One might argue that doing so addresses the problem I am raising here by bringing the analyst's character to center stage. Certainly, one's personal use of one's reactions to the patient is at the heart of our work, however we describe it; but in many case discussions in which the presenter alludes to her "countertransference," two trends seem to predominate.

First, the analyst uses the term to refer to her conscious experience of the patient, as if there were no unconscious transference to the patient. Second, the discussions often seem to assume that every analyst would have the same reaction to the patient. The extreme version of this view is the notion that whatever the analyst feels was somehow "put there" by the patient. If that is the analyst's stance, she will miss the contribution of her character to the process – and the analyst will teach those aspects of her own character that make her prone to certain countertransferences as though they were the generalizable technique of attending to "the" countertransference. A theory about using the countertransference may be invaluable, but it does not necessarily succeed in accounting for the uniqueness of the analyst's character in the analytic process.

It is not always so – talented teachers help their students find their own voices – but it is all too common. And students, desperate for a guiding light through the analytic wilderness, will be tempted to latch onto any certainty they can find and postpone the crucial realization that certainty has a stultifying effect on clinical work. Drs. A and P are splendid analysts but not gifted teachers. They try to codify their "techniques" based on what they do with patients that works, but their techniques work because of what they are able to hear through the filters of their own characters. They offer their students a valuable expansion of how to listen for what they (the teachers) hear, but the danger is that they imply that what the supervisor hears and does is the only important thing for the student to hear and do. They end up teaching their own characteristic language instead of helping supervisees refine their own language.

But clinical life is even more complex. Even the most basic principles devolve into something else when we look at them in action. Consider, for example, the principles "interpret from the surface" or "interpret at the point of urgency." These two principles have been debated as if they were opposed to each other. The former was associated with so-called "ego psychology," the latter with Kleinian thought.

But how does one locate the "surface" or the "point of urgency"? It is a fair bet that Drs. A and P would disagree in a given hour, but that is not simply a matter of theoretical allegiances. The so-called surface is not an aspect of the patient in isolation but the interface between patient and analyst as experienced by the analyst. The point of urgency is an affective judgment made by the analyst interacting with the patient. With a little reflection it becomes apparent that these principles are based on what the individual analyst hears in a given moment, and different analysts will be differently receptive.

Where Do Technical Principles Come From?

Friedman (e.g., 1988) has pioneered an approach to studying analysis by examining what analysts actually do, including how they theorize, and reasoning backward to the problems to which they were responding. Following his approach, we can draw inferences from articulated technical principles about the pressures the analyst faces in the clinical encounter. It is my impression that the most widely accepted principles of technique are variations on the theme of either making or managing a very personal connection to the patient. One such principle is about the optimal point of contact, such as interpret from the surface or at the point of urgency. The more basic premise that governs those directions is "follow the affect" – that is, notice what and where the patient is feeling. Each school also has some version of a technical direction about how to be affectively engaged.

Here we begin to see an oscillation between two positions. Freud's (1915) counsel of abstinence seemed to warn against a temptation for the analyst to become overinvolved or exploitive, but he also advised *against* interpreting the "conscious and unobjectionable" positive transference (Freud, 1912, p.106) in order not to disturb the emotional engagement that made the work possible. This formulation of the unanalyzed unobjectionable positive transference was the prototype of what would later be described by Greenson (1967) as the working alliance and by Zetzel (1970) as the therapeutic alliance. The assumption underlying the alliance concept is that it is possible to separate a rational and collaborative engagement between the parties from the passionate affair and battle between them. Kohut (1971) emphasized the role of empathy as a technique, while Winnicott (1960) and Bion (1962) brought us the concepts of the holding environment and the containing function. Klein's (1946) concept of projective identification, elaborated subsequently by Bion (1958), created a framework for passionate exchanges between analyst and patient that clearly attributed the source of the passions to the patient.

The coinage of the term "countertransference" did the same – it put the analyst's passions in a technical box separate both from "real" passions and from "transference" passions attributed to patients (see Part III). Developmentalists and attachment theorists brought us the concept of attunement. Schwaber (1992) insisted on listening from the patient's point of view. Many contemporary theorists favor an egalitarian stance for the analyst – or perhaps, more accurately, an anti-authoritarian stance.

All these positions have their merits, and each addresses a particular potential problem area in the analytic situation. But what I want to point out is that they all imply the need to deal with two contrary temptations the analyst faces: one toward uncritical love or merger, the other toward detachment.

This is a central function of defining a technique. We have "techniques" of engagement to overcome the danger of disengagement, of feeling no alliance, of being unempathic or unattuned, of neglecting the patient's experience, of being intolerant of the patient's emotions, and of failing to put the patient at the center of the process. At the same time, *codifying* our ways of engaging with patients into a "technique" with a special vocabulary also solves the opposite problem: It keeps patients at a safe distance and helps us manage the pull to merge with or exploit them. When we love or hate our patients, it is tolerable because we have ways of telling ourselves it is somehow not real; the feelings belong to technical empathy, or countertransference, or trial identification, or the reception of projective identification, or role-responsiveness (Sandler, 1976), or the "evocation of a proxy" (Wangh, 1962). These are all valuable concepts, but they also serve to give the analyst a little breathing room from the personal intensity of the work.

Clinical First Principles

It may be apparent from this list of technical recommendations that I am inferring an underlying principle common to all theoretical camps. The principle is that there must be a point of affective contact between patient and analyst, one that is both genuinely intense and bearable in its intensity. That interface determines the so-called analytic surface, or point of urgency, that is *accessible to both parties*. When an analyst "follows the affect," she is doing two different tasks in sequence: first, appreciating (or empathizing with, or enacting, or identifying with, or reliving, or accepting the projection of, or containing, or tuning into, or holding, or validating) an aspect of the patient's felt experience; second, considering the patient's experience from the position of an observer – to use Poland's (2000) terms, a witness and other, who brings an outsider's perspective to the experience. I will describe these two tasks more fully in Part IV.

Why should we feel the need to make this into a technical principle? Because no analyst has escaped the experience of being simply reactive to a patient and being unable to appreciate the patient's underlying motivations; and no analyst has escaped the experience of losing touch with the patient – as one senior analyst once put it: "Sometimes my evenly hovering attention floats right out the door." Even beyond the structural limits of psychoanalytic knowing, each of us comes up against her personal limitations. But curiously, we seem to feel that it should be otherwise. We do not readily accept that we will do our best and that at times it will not be enough; we tell ourselves that our professional limits are our moral failures. Worse, we attack our colleagues for what we fear are our own shortcomings.

The Function of Theoretical Schools

This indictment of our colleagues for failures we see in ourselves is one reason for the persistence of such intense group affiliations under theoretical banners. Another is what Freud (1930, p. 114) called the narcissism of minor differences. Perhaps the most important reason for group affiliation is the fear of being alone in a work situation that cannot be anything but alone. Our group affiliations are a way to tell ourselves that we are not doing anything crazy or criminal, that we are not giving in to the intense regressive pulls of our own primitive urges that the analytic situation stirs up.

We invite our patients to experience their most terrifying demons in a context in which we try to convey that it is safe to do so, but alone with a patient we do not always feel that safety ourselves. As analysts, we face two enormous temptations in the analytic situation: One is to give in to our sexual or aggressive desires, and the other is to withdraw in order to avoid giving in to our desires. Defining the analytic project as a matter of technique and allying oneself with a school are both ways to create relatively secure rules of engagement for the analytic situation while protecting the analyst from fears of losing self-control.

As I have already implied, my view of the divisions between theoretical groups is that they are based primarily on character traits. This applies to theories of development and models of the mind as much as to theories of technique. It would be silly to say that all self-psychologists want to be thought of as nice people, that all Kleinians want to be seen as tough enough to face the most primitively aggressive demons, that all "close process" ego psychologists want to be thought of as rational, that all intersubjectivists want to be seen as egalitarian, that all Lacanians want to be seen as intellectuals, and so on; yet the stereotypes are recognizable enough to imply that certain theories attract certain kinds of people.

What that says to me is that if we wanted a more accurate division of analysts into groups, we should sort them according to how they fall on certain character continua. For example, Drs. A and P are at opposite ends of the activity–passivity axis; we might also consider the rational–emotional axis, the strong–weak axis, the mind–body axis, the doubt–certainty axis, the simple–complex axis, the patience–impatience axis, the participant–observer axis, the rigidity–flexibility axis, or many others.

In fact, I think we already do that kind of categorizing informally. Consider how often referrals are made in the form of "He needs someone with a gentle touch," or "She needs someone who will stand up to her," or "He needs someone with the patience of Job," or "She needs somebody who won't try to compete with her."

The Relation of Theory to Clinical Practice

So far I have characterized theory in terms of its social and psychological function for the analyst. It is certainly true that theory is an important vehicle for raising questions and drawing distinctions in our work, but I have left myself open to the charge that I am underestimating the role of theory in shaping practice and in gaining precision in the way we approach our clinical work. Let me address one of the relevant questions directly: To what extent do our competing psychoanalytic theories of the mind differentiate our clinical decisions? Up to now I have argued that theory and technique are both largely selected and shaped by the analyst's character. But what about the profound disagreements among theoretical schools? Independent of the analyst's psychological needs, fundamental ideas may be right or wrong. How much of a clinical difference do those theoretical differences make?

My sense is that, with regard to at least some of the most hotly contested theoretical issues, they matter, but not as much as we think. Consider, for example, the nature of aggression. A good deal of heat has been generated over the years in an argument about whether aggression is a projection of the death instinct, a basic drive in its own right, or a reaction to frustration. These positions help distinguish the Kleinians, the Freudians since Hartmann, and the British object-relations independent group, respectively.

I would suggest that one can do a whole lot of clinical analysis without ever having to choose which of those alternatives is aggressive bedrock. At some point in an analysis, the distinction may come up in a meaningful way, but, if at that point our hypothetical paths diverge, does that invalidate all of the other work that has been done?

I am not arguing that these distinctions do not matter, just that, in the context of a whole analysis, it does not matter as much as our arguments would suggest. Clinically, we do not encounter drives or instincts; we come across desires and fantasies that we infer to be derivative. The substantive issues we face around aggression are, along with everything else, issues of the omnipotence of thought: Does the patient imagine magically dangerous consequences as the result of aggressive feelings, or of refraining from aggression? Does the patient alter her life in order to accommodate those fantasies? And so on. As far as I can tell, there is nothing in any of the theories that precludes that kind of exploration.

As I have suggested, it may be the case that an analyst of a given school will privilege one issue of aggression over another – the defensive use of aggression against frightening intimacy, say, or the destructive use of aggression motivated by envy – but one expects good clinicians to keep listening even after they find what their theories (and their characters) prefer. In fact, one danger common to all theories is that the analyst stops listening upon reaching the "bedrock" of the theory.

As a second example, consider the theories of the psychological "prime mover." Freud (1920) formulated Eros, under which libido was assumed, and the death instinct. Libido, according to Freud, could be directed toward an object or toward the ego (1914). Fairbairn (1963), in his outline of his version of object relations theory, stated that there is no id, that libido is a product of the ego, and that "the ego, and therefore libido, is fundamentally object-seeking" (p. 224). How does this major theoretical distinction matter in the clinical situation? Again, less than we might presume. I could not easily come up with an example where a clinician could discover, for example, autoerotic urges independent of real or fantasied objects.

I do not want to overstate the case – there are undoubtedly situations in which these distinctions come into play – but I suspect that, clinically, they are far less important than one would guess from the amount of heat they generate among analysts.

What is Gained and What is Lost

The gain of hanging onto rules of technique or identifying oneself with a theoretical group is that the analyst is able to keep her bearings and manage the anxieties that the analytic situation generates. That is not a small accomplishment; it was not an understatement when Freud (1937) called analysis one of the impossible professions. But there is a trade-off between construing the work as technical and making genuine contact with the patient. Also, if technical or theoretical devices are treated as canon law rather than as a temporary scaffolding to use while one's analytic identity is under construction, the analyst will condemn herself for the inevitable failure to live up to the tenets of the analytic church or blind herself to perceived shortcomings. The more religious one is about one's affiliation, the less freedom one has to discover one's own voice.

The point of affective contact with the patient is a personal matter, unique to the particular analyst–patient pair. That point is harder to achieve if the analyst thinks she has to hear and feel the same thing her teacher or supervisor does. In the optimal course of professional development, an analyst may begin as a Kleinian, or a self-psychologist, or an intersubjectivist, but ultimately the analyst should realize that one is of no school but one's own. The alternative is to become a robot. There is not much difference between an ego-psychological robot or a Kleinian robot or a Kohutian robot. Robots, after all, have interchangeable parts and the possibility of a technical manual to govern their operation. Humans, including patients and analysts, are not well described by technical manuals. We would do well to acknowledge in our clinical approach to patients that Harry Stack Sullivan's (1947) famous dictum applies to analysts as well as to patients: "We are all much more simply human than otherwise."

Implications for Teaching

Lipton's observation that "technique" in analysis should refer to the analyst's intentions rather than her behavior is as timely today as it was in 1977. What I have tried to do here is to pursue the implications of that realization a step further: The analyst's intentions, actualized through her unique character, imply that analytic technique is not generalizable. We can teach analytic theories – that is, models of how the mind develops and works; we can teach technical principles – that is, how minds interact in the clinical situation, how to expand our listening, and so on. Beyond that, we cannot and should not teach students to analyze the same way we do. Our task has to be to help candidates learn to respect who they are as clinicians, to become themselves in their clinical work.

References

Bion, W.R. (1958). On arrogance. *The International Journal of Psychoanalysis, 39*, 144–6.
Bion, W.R. (1962). *Learning from experience*. Heineman.
Fairbairn, W.R.D. (1963). Synopsis of an object-relations theory of the personality. *The International Journal of Psychoanalysis, 44*(2), 224–5.
Freud, S. (1912). The dynamics of transference. *SE 12*, 97–108.
Freud, S. (1914). On narcissism. An introduction. *SE 14*, 67–102.
Freud, S. (1915). Observations on transference-love (further recommendations on the technique of psycho-analysis III). *SE 12*, 163–4.
Freud, S. (1920). Beyond the pleasure principle. *SE 18*, 1–64.
Freud, S. (1930). Civilization and its discontents. *SE 21*, 114.
Freud, S. (1937). Analysis terminable and interminable. *SE 23*, 209–54.
Friedman, L. (1988). *The anatomy of psychotherapy*. The Analytic Press.
Gorman, H.E. (2008). An intention-based definition of psychoanalytic attitude: What does it look like? How does it grow? *The Psychoanalytic Review, 95*(5), 751–76.
Greenson, R.R. (1967). *The technique and practice of psychoanalysis*. International Universities Press.
Hoffman, I.Z. (1994). Dialectical thinking and therapeutic action in the psychoanalytic process. *The Psychoanalytic Quarterly, 63*(2), 187–218.

Klein, M. (1946). Notes on some schizoid mechanisms. *The International Journal of Psychoanalysis, 27*, 99–110.

Kohut, H. (1971). *The analysis of the self*. International Universities Press.

Lipton, S.D. (1977). The advantages of Freud's technique as shown in his analysis of the rat-man. *The International Journal of Psychoanalysis, 58*(3), 255–73.

Poland, W.S. (2000). The analyst's witnessing and otherness. *Journal of the American Psychoanalytic Association, 48*(1), 17–34.

Poland, W.S. (2002). The interpretive attitude. *Journal of the American Psychoanalytic Association, 50*(3), 807–26.

Renik, O. (1993a). Analytic interaction: Conceptualizing technique in light of the analyst's irreducible subjectivity. *The Psychoanalytic Quarterly, 62*, 553–71.

Renik, O. (1993b). Countertransference enactment and the psychoanalytic process. In M.J. Horowitz, O.F. Kernberg, & E.M. Weinshel (Eds.), *Psychic structure and psychic change: Essays in honor of Robert S. Wallerstein, M.D.* (pp. 135–58). International Universities Press.

Sandler, J. (1976) Countertransference and role-responsiveness. *International Review of Psycho-Analysis, 3*(1), 43–7.

Schwaber, E.A. (1992). Countertransference: The analyst's retreat from the patient's vantage point. *The International Journal of Psychoanalysis, 73*(2), 349–61.

Sullivan, H.S. (1947). *Conceptions of modern psychiatry*. Norton.

Wangh, M. (1962). The "evocation of a proxy": A psychological maneuver, its use as a defense, its purposes and genesis. *The Psychoanalytic Study of the Child, 17*, 451–69.

Winnicott, D.W. (1960). The theory of the parent-infant relationship. *International Journal of Psychoanalysis, 41*, 585–95.

Zetzel, E. (1970). *The capacity for emotional growth*. International Universities Press.

Part III

Empathy and Countertransference

I see it feelingly.

(King Lear [IV, 6])

In the analytic encounter, as in ordinary conversation, each person discerns the meaning, intended and unintended, that the other conveys. Although we call that process *listening*, it is much more complex than, say, reading a transcript of the spoken words. We filter an amalgam of spoken language, rhythm, intonation, facial expression, body language and other sense data, and context through our own expectations, fears, and desires, and we experience thoughts and feelings of our own from which we intuit a meaning. Most of that process takes place rapidly and unconsciously. When we turn our attention to the particular experience leading to the intuition, we may attribute it to empathy or to countertransference.

In Chapter 14 I give a brief clinical example of so-called countertransference and its partial analysis. I argue that the distinction between empathy and countertransference can only be made retrospectively, and it is never simple. I suggest that empathy begins with transference to the patient – as all interpersonal connections begin with transference.

Chapter 15 is a more elaborate discussion of the concept of countertransference. I review a historical summary by Sander Abend, published in 1980, and note the changing views of the role of the analyst in the analytic process. I try to develop the point that the term *countertransference* is misleading and is used defensively to avoid recognition of the analyst's transference to the patient. Along the way I note and applaud the disappearance of the concept of the "mainstream" analyst.

DOI: 10.4324/9781003360391-17

Chapter 14

Empathy and "Countertransference"

A Jewish man in analysis used a Yiddish expression, which he immediately translated into English. "I don't know why I have to translate for you," he went on; "I know you're Jewish." (In fact, he was not sure.) I said to him, "You try not to think of me as family." He immediately agreed, going on to say how some American Jews don't speak Yiddish, but his family does. This led to a new angle on a familiar theme in our work, which was his emphasis on in-groups and out-groups. The new material had to do with how he used his sense of exclusion, as well as his sense of being one of the Chosen, as a way to rationalize his various distancing maneuvers.

The patient's immediate experience of my comment was to feel connected to me. It seemed that my remark let him consider why he needed to exclude me, and for the moment why he needed to refrain from doing so. But besides the apparent correctness of my remark, I subsequently learned that he had heard my phrasing, and even the cadence of my speech, as Jewish. I was confirming that I was family, at least for the moment, without intentionally either affirming or denying my Yiddish-speaking status.

In fact, when I started to speak, I had been about to use the Hebrew word *mespocheh* instead of "family"; without knowing why, I had changed it at the last moment. In retrospect, it was clear to me that I had wanted to use the Hebrew word to prove I knew it and to compete with him in Yiddish knowledge – a subject about which I feel inferior. I was going to "prove" I was family – not to be connected but to outdo him, to prove I was in the in-group.

My actual comment was not free of those motives either. Even my changing the word had elements of competition and dis-identification in it – strategies I hadn't realized I had in common with my patient: I was saying "I'm not like you, I am better; I don't have to show off to outdo you!" As I considered some of my own motives, I became more aware of some of the subtle ways in which the patient hid his competitive strivings behind mild one-upmanship. I noticed these maneuvers in reviewing earlier interactions, although I found it impossible to sort out which of us had initiated it; it was

DOI: 10.4324/9781003360391-18

a style of conversation between us, a shared language, with mutual deference and respect concealing the tiniest exchange of barbs.

My revised remark still contained the hidden edge – if not in the words, then in the tone or rhythm. But it also contained other motives, including the effort to be helpful, and at least a degree of awareness of his sensitivity to being excluded – a sensitivity based in part on his projected wish to exclude.

I did not plan in any orderly way either to compete with him or to accommodate his touchiness in this area. (Looking back, I have never found that even those few interventions that I thought I had "planned" conveyed simply what I intended.)

As I thought about my change of word, and my state of mind as best I could retrieve it, I recalled an incident from my childhood, on the eve of my older brother's Bar Mitzvah. As he was being celebrated by my parents, I had sought to steal some of his thunder by showing off my expertise, and my brother's ignorance, in some area of science. My parents had seen through the ploy and had dismissed me, leaving me feeling ashamed about the attempt. But my brother responded in a way that surprised me: He was interested and asked me to tell him more about my topic.

I had the feeling that my brother understood my sense of exclusion; by his show of interest, he had created a club of him and me. This was especially unusual to me at the time. What had seemed a more typical interaction between us was his not letting me join his club some time earlier, to which I had responded by announcing that I would form my own club.

My initial reaction to my patient's translation was to feel excluded and to want to turn the tables, but, in the moment of changing the word, I spoke as my older brother to the younger brother who needed to have his own club in which to be a member. I think I had heard my own childhood voice in his tone. This interaction got me started on a reconsideration of what I came to realize had been a caricatured view of my brother and how we had gotten along. It also alerted me to the fact that my patient's picture of his brother was similarly two dimensional, emphasizing the competition and ignoring the warmth and caring that he found threatening.

Recent psychoanalytic thinking has begun to take full account of the major role that "countertransference" plays in the analytic process. Contributions by Jacobs (1986) and others have alerted us to the ways in which even our "correct" technique may (I would say, *must*) enact the "countertransference." In this commonplace example, my competitive motives are clearly based on a view of interactions persisting from a childhood interpretation of events. But what I wish to emphasize is that my compassionate, empathic action was also rooted in the reenactment of a childhood experience. It was not simply a recognition of the patient's experience; it was a reliving of a congruent experience of my own. Although recognition adds a new dimension to reliving and reduces its compulsive power, I do not believe that recognition occurs without reliving. The subsequent experience must amalgamate both.

From my description above, my view may become clear that what we like to call "countertransference" is simply the analyst's transference to the patient. So why do we need a separate term? I think analysts need to find ways to distance themselves from the heat of the transference action. Having a term reserved exclusively for the analyst is a way of asserting a difference, and therefore a distance, from the patient's struggles.

The fact that I believe I had gone through something akin to the patient's experience is not evidence that I was right; in fact, much of what we now commonly understand as countertransference is the analyst's jumping to a conclusion based on her own transference expectations.

Renik (1993) has argued persuasively against the assumption that "countertransference" fantasy can become conscious without first having been expressed in action, however subtle that action may be. We expect our patients to enact their transferences as a precondition of becoming aware of them; the same is true for the analyst's transference. I agree with Renik's conclusion that the analyst's psychology expressed in action is not only inevitable but a useful part of the analytic process and it can only be understood retrospectively.

I intend my clinical report to illustrate how it is only in retrospect that we can partially distinguish empathic intuition from transference to the patient. Empathy is a name applied to the judgment (after the fact) that what we felt fit the patient's experience. In order to feel it, we must draw on our own experience; in order to understand it, we must examine the feeling in retrospect.

The role of the analyst's transference ("the countertransference") to the patient is confused by our tendency to see it as an obstacle to be surmounted. But it is a fact of the interaction, and it is not available for consideration until it has been put into action. Transference, in the sense of the set of personal *a priori* expectations applied to a new situation, is the vehicle for entering into relations with another person. It is our initial frame of reference, to be reconsidered in light of our subsequent experience. It is neither an obstacle to the relationship nor a fact about the other person; it is a condition for the beginning of a relationship that is constantly redefined by the participants.

Empathy is not something to be sought after, and "countertransference" is not something to be avoided. Each term refers to what the analyst *feels* while trying to engage in as genuine a way as possible. Neither is a problem in itself, although the effort to avoid or ignore any feeling one has about the patient is problematic. Both belong to the realm of participating, and they are subject to judgment only after stepping out of the action to observe it. After that, events may lead the therapist to ask herself: To what extent am I feeling with the patient (empathy)? And to what extent am I seeing the patient through my own fears and wishes (transference)?

References

Jacobs, T.J. (1986). On countertransference enactments. *Journal of the American Psychoanalytic Association, 34*(2), 289–307.

Renik, O. (1993). Countertransference enactment and the psychoanalytic process. In M.J. Horowitz, O.F. Kernberg, & E.M. Weinshel (Eds.), *Psychic structure and psychic change. Essays in honor of Robert S. Wallerstein, M.D.* (pp. 135–58). International Universities Press.

Chapter 15

The Person in the Analyst's Chair

The ongoing evolution of thinking about the use of the analyst's self probably began with Freud's (1912) image of the analyst turning his unconscious as a receptive organ toward the patient's transmitting unconscious. In the 1950s, the role of the self-as-analyst took the form of the countertransference debate. In the 1980s, the discussion most often took the form of the analyst's role in the psychoanalytic process. I believe that the next version of the topic should be the role of the analyst's character in the process.

In this chapter I will review the history of the countertransference debate as a way to look at the shift in emphasis away from thinking of analyzing the patient's narrative and toward thinking of analyzing shared action. I will then turn to the increasingly serious consideration of the role of the analyst's character in her work. In closing I will return to the countertransference argument itself and expand on the view I introduced in the last chapter.

The Analyst as Catalyst: Context and Consequences of the Debate

In the space of three years (1949–51), Winnicott, Heimann, and Racker articulated views of using what they called the countertransference in analysis (Abend, 1989). The three papers met substantial opposition among "mainstream" (that is, largely American ego-psychologist) analysts. The arguments for each position were thoughtful and well reasoned, if heated – except that the dismissiveness of each group toward the other meant that neither took up the fundamental assumptions underlying the differences between the positions. Discussions of how and why the models of the mind and its development differed, and how they overlapped, were rare.

In the 1960s, some British Kleinians began to visit (and, in some cases, join) the Los Angeles Psychoanalytic Society and Institute. Discussions there between the Kleinians and the Freudians were typically uncivil and often stormy, to the point where the American Psychoanalytic Association felt compelled to intervene. Arguments would end in a kind of stalemate, with the Kleinians saying they worked with sicker patients, while privately they would

DOI: 10.4324/9781003360391-19

imply that the Freudians were dealing with trivial problems. The Freudians would say they demanded more of their patients, while privately dismissing the Kleinians as not doing analysis.[1] In extreme cases, some analysts privately called their opponents psychopaths (Reeder, 2004, p. 181).

Boesky (2008) called this the "era of the hegemony of structural theory" (p. xi). Not only did the mainstream group of analysts, centered mainly in the US, dismiss the British Kleinians and middle group, they largely ignored what would come to be known as the relational perspective in America, whose institutes were barred from participation in the American and International Psychoanalytic associations. Within the former, Stone's (e.g., 1961) humanistic concerns were attacked and/or dismissed by mainstream analysts (see, e.g., Brenner, 1979). The work of Hans Loewald, whose thinking offered a substantial integration of Freudian, object relations, developmental and relational theories, was largely ignored by the mainstream, as well as by the British schools.

According to Abend (1989), remarkably enough, something useful to all came from the countertransference argument: "The original Kleinian proposition that analysts' emotional reactions to patients can be a source of increased understanding of patients' material has become accepted in all quarters" (p. 391). "Increased clinical acuity characterized both sides of the theoretical debate. Improvement of our understanding of various manifestations of countertransference has continued to the present day" (Abend, 1989, p. 385). And, perhaps more importantly, "it has been helpful to us in our work, and in our discussions, to make countertransference a respectable subject for study .... [T]he creation of an institutionalized dedication to acknowledging the unavoidability of countertransference ... seems to have gradually had a beneficial effect, encouraging greater honesty, acceptance, and probably an improvement in clinical skills" (Abend, 1989, p. 389).

Considering the theoretical territoriality that characterizes our field to the present day, this was good news indeed. It is my impression that the greater honesty that Abend attributed to the countertransference debate has led to greater openness about theoretical premises, a greater willingness to show our actual clinical work, and our continuing interest in the psychoanalytic process, to which Abend contributed in his 1989 paper. I believe Abend is among the first from within the narrowly defined mainstream to acknowledge this shift in mainstream thinking.

The two sides of the original countertransference debate share the assumption that the analyst is ideally a catalyst – that is, the analyst's presence makes things happen without "contaminating" (much less being changed by) the process. In the American view of that era, countertransference is contamination; in the British version, countertransference is something received entirely from the patient, without the analyst putting anything of herself into the mix.

The assumption, not completely unquestioned but also not thoroughly studied before the 1980s, was the idea that the analyst could somehow be bracketed out of consideration of the patient's world. The countertransference debate of the 1950s did not challenge this assumption but laid it bare for future reconsideration.

A second assumption, which Abend began to question in the context of the countertransference debate, is that the analyst's theoretical position describes the analyst's clinical work. I will pursue these in turn, as the analyst *acting* and the analyst *being*.

The Analyst Acting: What Do We Mean by Technique?

Many years ago I proposed a panel to the Program Committee of the American Psychoanalytic Association's meeting, to be called "Modes of Influence in Analysis." The first reaction to the proposal was by a highly respected analyst who said: "We don't influence our patients" (personal communication, 1993). This reflexive response captures something of the tenor of the times of Abend's paper, at least within institutes of the American Psychoanalytic Association. It is consistent with Abend's acceptance of what he cited as "Freud's opinion that the analyst should not seek to influence the patient's neurosis except through the medium of interpretation" (Abend, 1989, p. 377).

Abend also pointed out on the same page that Freud's early view of neurosis was as a circumscribed illness within an otherwise healthy personality; perhaps that is why Freud felt free to influence the *patient* – as distinct from the patient's *neurosis* – in a variety of noninterpretive ways, e.g., by exploiting rather than interpreting the "unobjectionable" transference (1912, p. 105) or by reassuring the patient of his good opinion (1909, p. 178). Lipton (1977) made the observation that Freud's technique in the Rat Man case did not contradict his emphasis on interpretation precisely because Freud did not think of his noninterpretive activity as a technical intervention. Lipton argued that there is no evidence that Freud's technique ever changed after the 1909 case (I think Abend would disagree). Lipton went on to point out that Ernst Kris's (1951) reading of the Rat Man case effectively (and, in Lipton's view, incorrectly) redefined the meaning of technique from the analyst's *purposes* to the analyst's *behavior* (Lipton, 1977, p. 258).

From the end of the war until the time of Abend's paper, the American Psychoanalytic Association was synonymous with mainstream analysis in the United States. The prevailing view of technique of that group was that the analyst was to *do nothing* but interpret (note the emphasis on the analyst's behavior, rather than purpose);[2] presumably, being silent and listening respectfully were oddly equated with doing nothing. An important aspect of this view is captured in an old joke:

A kind-hearted farmer wanted to train his very stubborn mule, but he was troubled by the aversive techniques that were in vogue. Then he saw an ad from a mule trainer who used "affection training." He hired the man, who confirmed that he used only affection in his work. Then the trainer picked up a length of 2x4 lumber and slammed the mule on the side of the head. The farmer was horrified and cried, "What are you doing?" The trainer replied, "First you have to get their attention."

If technique is defined in terms of behavior, then every theory of technique will have its 2x4s – those necessary but undocumented ways to position both participants to enable the interpretive work. Like the mule trainer, we just don't count those actions as part of our technique. This allows us, for example, to treat being silent as if it is doing nothing. It also allows us to read any instance of the analyst's "doing something" as a countertransference interference – or, at best, as a "parameter" to be analyzed subsequently.[3] As Lipton argued, this was not Freud's view, since Freud's idea of technique referred to the analyst's purpose rather than behavior.

I suspect that this general approach worked well enough for a long time because it was supported by case selection. Freud, after all, saw analysis as a treatment for neurosis. The structural model helped clarify the concept of neurosis in terms of intrapsychic conflict involving a relatively "intact" ego (i.e., one that is not prone to severe regression), and the mainstream became known as ego psychology.[4] I believe most, if not all, of the institutes of the American Psychoanalytic Association had committees to assess the "analyzability" of potential cases for training. A narrow view of who was suitable for analysis may have inadvertently selected for patients who were able to adapt to their analysts' idiosyncrasies and make good use of them,[5] and, as I suggested earlier, I imagine every analyst has an armamentarium of extra-theoretical 2x4s. But by the mid-1950s the scope of indications for analysis had widened to include more non-neurotic conditions (Stone, 1954).

Abend noted that experience from the treatment of sicker patients, especially by the Kleinians, helped to kindle the interest in using countertransference as information about patients. He mentioned in passing that their theoretical focus on projective identification and introjection probably led to their "emphasis on how one individual can be made to feel something by another" (Abend, 1989, p. 380). I think this formulation probably reverses cause and effect. It seems more likely to me that the clinical experience of being "made to feel something" by the more disturbed patients (and the children) they were treating led the Kleinians to formulate a theory that included a revision in the understanding of countertransference – and also of projective identification (see, for example, Malin & Grotstein, 1966).

More important for my purpose is Abend's observation that the Kleinians were interested, circa 1950, in the question of "how one individual can be made to feel something by another." If we consider the broader meaning of that question (beyond the specifics of defining countertransference), we are now in the realm of how people influence each other. I imagine that raising this issue revealed more plainly than before the untenable position that the patient's and analyst's minds followed different sets of rules. Although not tackled directly in the early countertransference debates, the need to get rid of that contradiction has reshaped contemporary explorations of the psychoanalytic process. At the time, neither the mainstream view that countertransference was the analyst's problem nor the view of Heimann and other followers of Klein that everything the analyst experienced was something created by the patient addressed the role of mutual interaction as something to be analyzed.

Again, in the narrower context of the countertransference discussion, Jacobs (1986) reminded us that we are always doing something besides exchanging verbal signifiers. At the same time, Betty Joseph (1985), writing from a Kleinian perspective, called our attention to transference as "how [the patient] is using the analyst, alongside and beyond what he is saying" (p. 447). Despite her view of transference, Joseph seems to have accepted the view of countertransference as the patient's creation – a version of the analyst as catalyst.

Earlier in the decade, Hoffman (1983), Gill (1983), and Greenberg (1981) published critiques of the concept of neutrality that helped refine the role of the analyst's activity and personhood in the analytic process. Over time we have seen the evolution of the text to be analyzed as, first, the patient's narrative (as Freud might have analyzed a dream); second, the patient's action, including speech as action ("Here is what I think you are doing with me"); and, finally, the interaction ("Here is what I think we have been doing"). Attention to all three keeps us from ruling out potentially valuable information and experience.

One of the legacies of the countertransference debate was expanding our clinical data to include the possibility of attending to the interaction in a way that enriches our work immeasurably. The shift of emphasis that was taking place in the 1980s was leading away from the idea that the analyst might inadvertently depart from analysis and enact something and toward the view that we need to attend to the fact that patient and analyst are *always* enacting something together (Renik, 1993, p. 556).

The idea of "enactment," or transference–countertransference action, was not a brand-new idea, but it seems to have needed rediscovery and reemphasis. Boesky (1982, 1990) revisited it in the 1980s. What was novel, at least for the mainstream, was the emphasis on the analyst's participation in action – for example, in Boesky's (1990)[6] position that *"the manifest form of a resistance is even sometimes unconsciously negotiated by both patient and analyst"* (p. 572; italics in original).

As to Abend's direct contributions to that discussion, for the most part, they took the appropriate form of questions and uncertainties. "We are still puzzled and intrigued by the mysterious processes by means of which analysts understand the meaning of their patients' unconscious productions, and still hard pressed to give a good account of how we arrive at our judgments" (Abend, 1989, p. 388). Toward the end of the paper, he wrote:

> At the present time there is an active focus of theoretical and technical
> dispute about certain unverbalized and unverbalizable aspects of the emo-
> tional interaction between analyst and patient. Are these integral parts
> of the analytic experience? Can they be formulated systematically for
> some classes of patient, or perhaps even for all patients? Should the ana-
> lyst conceive of his or her therapeutic role as including these nonverbal
> dimensions or not?
>
> (Abend, 1989, p. 391)

To Abend's question about the role of the unverbalized in analysis, I would
agree with Loewald's (1979) observation that whether we address those silent
processes is a clinical judgment. It may be the case that, with some neurotic
patients, the atmosphere of safety, of caring engagement, of respect, of privacy
"go without saying" until a relatively encapsulated departure emerges and can
be addressed. But with other (especially non-neurotic) patients, we may not
be able to take any of those features for granted. We may have to give them
our explicit attention right from the beginning. We may have to use who we
are to help shape or reshape the structures that the structural model describes.
We do not act as surrogate parents, but we attend to work that we usually do
without noticing – work that is not parenting but has something in common
with parenting (Loewald, 1960).

It is not my goal to describe such work here. Rather, it is to point out that
such ideas, seen even in 1989 as departures from the mainstream, have begun
to be incorporated more generally into analytic thinking in recent years.
The variety of approaches to what we might call the two-person problem
has contributed to theoretical pluralism. But the idea that structure building
may be an integral part of the analytic process seems to be following an arc of
accommodation similar to the one that Abend described for useful attention
to countertransference.

The Analyst Being: Character and Technique

In making the point that the analyst's character and psychological makeup
determine what the analyst hears and does, Abend wrote: "The clinical distinctions analysts reach are inevitably subjective, individualistic,
variable .... This is so *even among colleagues of comparable training and theoretical
convictions*" (Abend, 1989, p. 386; emphasis added).

Abend arrived at this proposition via Brenner's formulation that all mental
life, whether in the patient or the analyst, consists of compromise formations
that may be useful, problematic, or indifferent. But the implication of the
quoted observation goes much further. It suggests that analysts are more
accurately grouped by their psychological makeup than by their theoretical allegiances (see Chapter 13), even allowing that individual psychology
determines group affiliations.

Consider one such sorting of analysts by character. We might call them the scientists and the artists.[7] Some analysts ("scientists") place a strong emphasis on propositional evidence, on cognitive validation; to borrow terms from laboratory testing (and mix a metaphor), their view of analysis might be said to be high in specificity in considering what issues to take up with patients. Others ("artists") place a strong emphasis on feeling reactions, on affective validation; their view might be said to be high in sensitivity.

Abend wrote: "The further one departs from verbal material, the more one relies on one's emotional responses to nonverbal dimensions of the interactions with patients, the more difficult the challenge of verification seems to become" (Abend, 1989, p. 392). This is undoubtedly true – although the question of "verification" has not been settled for verbal interactions either. Abend noted his discomfort with "mystical explanations of unconscious communication" (Abend, 1989, p. 388). I find the idea of using words to convey meaning from one mind to another every bit as mysterious.

For the scientists, Abend's statement is an implicit condemnation of the artists' willingness to settle for the "unverifiable" affective data (low specificity); for the artists, the statement is an implicit condemnation of the scientists' willingness to limit themselves to what is cognitively verifiable (low sensitivity). One might guess that the scientists would incline toward a narrower definition of analysis, the artists to a wider one; that the artists would be more inclined to work with sicker patients, the scientists to work with healthier ("intact") ones. Analysis requires its practitioners to be both artists and scientists, but an individual analyst will be more one than the other.

As Abend pointed out, the insistence that one is infallible, which he discussed as a proneness to authoritarianism, is a danger regardless of one's position; it "makes for bad analysts, and bad analyses, *irrespective of the theories that inform such an individual's technique*" (Abend, 1989, p. 390; emphasis added). As Reed (1987) put it: "Indoctrination remains indoctrination regardless of the doctrine." This is another affirmation of the principle that a *character trait*, authoritarianism, says more about how an analyst works than does her theoretical affiliation. Although character considerations inevitably influence theorizing and theoretical affiliation, character traits cross theoretical lines, and it is my impression that they are more reflective of what the analyst actually does than espoused theories.

I have elaborated these ideas in Chapter 13 and will not repeat them here. I would point out, though, how the primacy of character over theory seems to be a common intuition among analysts, even though it is rarely addressed.[8] Consider how we make referrals. I mentioned the controversy between Brenner and Stone above. They were both mainstream analysts and members of the New York Psychoanalytic Society. Yet their temperamental differences are obvious. Malcolm (1982) describes Brenner as an "intransigent purist," "aseptic," "hard-line" (p. 4), "austere," "icy" (p. 45). She describes Stone as "humanistic," "of manifest good will" (p. 42), "humane," "flexible" (p. 44).

When considering what the patient needs, I believe a referring analyst thinks first not about the treating analyst's theoretical allegiance but about what kind of person she is (and what kind of couple the patient and analyst will be together). Even pairs of collaborators are separable by character types, despite their shared theoretical outlooks. With a specific patient in mind, many referrers would have a clear choice between co-authors Arlow and Brenner, or between Calef and Weinshel, or between Greenberg and Mitchell.

Pursuing this realization should put theoretical loyalties in a new context: Analysts can be sorted more accurately according to how they actually work, as demonstrated above all by what kind of people they are. I believe this is implied by Poland's (2002) adage, "Technique is attitude actualized" (p. 807). Attitudes are not encoded in theories; it is possible to be an impatient self-psychologist or a stingy intersubjectivist, an active ego psychologist or a generous Kleinian. Theories can be examined for the clinical problems they were invented to solve,[9] and the new honesty that Abend described can lead us to a view that, to paraphrase Sullivan (1930), we are all more simply analytic than otherwise.

Countertransference: One Contemporary View

In light of the above considerations, I will not resist the urge to return briefly to the specifics of the countertransference debate.

Abend's paper traced the evolution of the idea of countertransference from Freud's limited use as an obstacle to listening through the rise of using countertransference as information about the patient. He concluded with the observation of the general acceptance and enriching effect of attending to the analyst's reactions to the patient, as noted above. He also commented that, although there are still (circa 1989) arguments about the term, common usage has settled *de facto* on the definition of countertransference as all of the analyst's reactions to the patient (Abend, 1989, p. 383). He did not seem happy with that outcome, and neither are those of us who have continued the discussion (see, for example, Chapter 14; also Renik, 1993; Wilson, 2013).

Today I think Heimann's position may retain the most influence internationally; yet Abend's synopsis (Abend, 1989, p. 378) shows readily why it is problematic. If countertransference consists of all feelings the analyst has toward the patient, and it is the patient's creation, and patients' and analysts' minds follow the same rules, then why do we not conclude that all feelings the patient has toward the analyst are the analyst's creation? Or (as I suggested in the previous chapter) have we held on to the term in order to gain a measure of safe distance from the patient through the implication that the mind of the analyst is governed by different principles than that of the patient?

This conjecture runs counter to Abend's tentative conclusion that a social egalitarian trend has contributed to the revision of thinking about countertransference (Abend, 1989, p. 381). Neither Heimann's Kleinian position nor A. Reich's "classical" position would be construed as egalitarian; each sees only one participant as having a "countertransference."

In our historical survey, one obvious question went unaddressed: Why did Freud choose to name "countertransference" as an obstacle to listening? Loewald (1986) wrote: "The word countertransference indicates that it is a *transferential* phenomenon" (p. 277; italics in original). As far as I can tell, Freud did not take up the issue; nowhere in his discussion of countertransference does the word transference appear. But does the term countertransference itself make any sense if it is not related to transference?

At this point in our evolution, I think the following statements should be relatively noncontroversial. First, we must account for the fact that the psychology that governs human nature applies to both patient and analyst. Second, what we call "transference" is a complex inference about unconscious expectations of what other people will be like; indeed, without it we might be unprepared to make contact with others at all (Loewald, 1960). Third, there is no interaction that is free of unconscious motives (or, as Abend and Brenner would prefer, that is not a compromise formation); therefore, there is no interaction that is free of transference.

With these three propositions in mind, the logical alternative is to drop the term countertransference because it is superfluous and misleading. If Abend's observation of the common parlance definition is correct, we should replace the phrase "my countertransference was ..." with "I felt ...." The analyst's imposition of her unconscious needs and expectations upon the patient should be called the analyst's transference (McLaughlin, 1981; note also Chapter 14). And obstacles to analytic listening should be called obstacles to analytic listening, without having to make an *a priori* judgment as to their sources. Abend quoted A. Reich: "Countertransference thus comprises the effects of the analyst's own unconscious needs on his understanding and technique" (Abend, 1989, p. 379). Since that is manifested in the interaction (i.e., understanding *of the patient*; technique of interacting *with the patient*), how does that differ from the analyst's transference? And how can it not be in play?

Concluding Remarks

The countertransference debate that began in the 1950s carried within it the seeds of two trends, both of which exemplify the role of the self of the analyst in the analytic process: a renewed emphasis on the analyst's unavoidable (in my view, nonstop) noninterpretive action, and an increased attention paid to the irreducible role of the analyst's character on her work. Most simply put, our theories are struggling openly now with ways to account for the analyst always acting, and the analyst always being who she is.

Notes

1 Janet Malcolm's (1982) pseudonymous New York mainstream analyst Aaron Green refers to the "Kleinian heresy" (p. 135).
2 The awkwardness of this position led Eissler (1953) to try to buy the analyst a little breathing room with his formulation of "parameters" (p. 110).
3 In a vein similar to the "2x4" story, Greenberg (1981) wrote, "Surely Brenner must do something to convince his patients that he is worth talking to ... but he is not about to tell us what that is, because no activity of the analyst beyond interpretation fits into his theory" (p. 245).
4 David Rapaport, one of the architects of ego psychology, dismissed the views of Klein and her followers as "id mythology" (1958).
5 It may be that the inability of children to make those adaptations might have contributed to the insistence in some circles that child analysis wasn't analysis.
6 I tend to think that this paper marked the end of the mainstream. Not everyone got the memo.
7 Ogden (2001) comments on a similar division (p. 321).
8 An exception is Kantrowitz's (1995) work on the patient–analyst match.
9 See Friedman (1988) for the pioneering work on this question.

References

Abend, S.M. (1989). Countertransference and psychoanalytic technique. *The Psychoanalytic Quarterly, 58*(3), 374–95.

Boesky, D. (1982). Acting out: A reconsideration of the concept. *The International Journal of Psychoanalysis, 63*(1), 39–55.

Boesky, D. (1990). The psychoanalytic process and its components. *The Psychoanalytic Quarterly, 59*(4), 550–84.

Boesky, D. (2008). *Psychoanalytic disagreements in context.* Jason Aronson.

Brenner, C. (1979). Working alliance, therapeutic alliance, and transference. *Journal of the American Psychoanalytic Association, 27*(Suppl.), 137–57.

Eissler, K.R. (1953). The effect of the structure of the ego on psychoanalytic technique. *Journal of the American Psychoanalytic Association, 1*, 104–43.

Freud, S. (1909). Notes upon a case of obsessional neurosis. SE *10*, 153–318.

Freud, S. (1912). The dynamics of transference. SE *12*, 97–108.

Friedman, L. (1988). *The anatomy of psychotherapy.* Analytic Press.

Gill, M.M. (1983). The interpersonal paradigm and the degree of the therapist's involvement. *Contemporary Psychoanalysis, 19*(2), 200–37.

Greenberg, J.R. (1981). Prescription or description: The therapeutic action of psychoanalysis. *Contemporary Psychoanalysis, 17*(2), 239–57.

Hoffman, I.Z. (1983). The patient as interpreter of the analyst's experience. *Contemporary Psychoanalysis, 19*(3), 389–422.

Jacobs, T.J. (1986). On countertransference enactments. *Journal of the American Psychoanalytic Association, 34*(2), 289–307.

Joseph, B. (1985). Transference: The total situation. *The International Journal of Psychoanalysis, 66*(4), 447–54.

Kantrowitz, J.L. (1995). The beneficial aspects of the patient-analyst match. *The International Journal of Psychoanalysis, 76*(2), 299–313.

Kris, E. (1951). Ego psychology and interpretation in psychoanalytic therapy. *The Psychoanalytic Quarterly, 20*, 15–30.

Lipton, S.D. (1977). The advantages of Freud's technique as shown in his analysis of the Rat Man. *The International Journal of Psychoanalysis, 58*(3), 255–73.

Loewald, H.W. (1952). The problem of defense and the neurotic interpretation of reality. *The International Journal of Psychoanalysis, 33*, 444–9.

Loewald, H.W. (1960). On the therapeutic action of psycho-analysis. *The International Journal of Psychoanalysis, 41*, 16–33.

Loewald, H.W. (1979). Reflections on the psychoanalytic process and its therapeutic potential. *The Psychoanalytic Study of the Child, 34*, 155–67.

Loewald, H.W. (1986). Transference-countertransference. *Journal of the American Psychoanalytic Association, 34*(2), 275–87.

Malcolm, J. (1982). *Psychoanalysis: The impossible profession.* Vintage.

Malin, A., & Grotstein, J.S. (1966). Projective identification in the therapeutic process. *The International Journal of Psychoanalysis, 47*(1), 26–31.

McLaughlin, J.T. (1981). Transference, psychic reality, and counter-transference. *The Psychoanalytic Quarterly, 50*, 639–64.

Ogden, T.H. (2001). Reading Winnicott. *The Psychoanalytic Quarterly, 70*(2), 299–323.

Poland, W.S. (2002). The interpretive attitude. *Journal of the American Psychoanalytic Association, 50*(3), 807–26.

Rapaport, D. (1958). An historical survey of psychoanalytic ego psychology. *Bulletin of the Philadelphia Association for Psychoanalysis, 8*(4), 105–20.

Reed, G.S. (1987). Rules of clinical understanding in classical psychoanalysis and in self psychology: A comparison. *Journal of the American Psychoanalytic Association, 35*(2), 421–46.

Reeder, J. (2004). *Hate and love in psychoanalytical institutions: The dilemma of a profession.* Other Press.

Renik, O. (1993). Analytic interaction: conceptualizing technique in light of the analyst's irreducible subjectivity. *The Psychoanalytic Quarterly, 62*(4), 553–71.

Stone, L. (1954). The widening scope of indications for psychoanalysis. *Journal of the American Psychoanalytic Association, 2*, 567–94.

Stone, L. (1961). *The psychoanalytic situation.* International Universities Press.

Sullivan, H.S. (1930). *Schizophrenia as a human process.* Norton (1962).

Sullivan, H.S. (1953). *The interpersonal theory of psychiatry* (H.S. Perry & M.L. Gawel, Eds.). W.W. Norton.

Wilson, M. (2013). Desire and responsibility: The ethics of the countertransference experience. *The Psychoanalytic Quarterly, 82*(2), 435–76.

Part IV

Acting and Reflecting

Who can be wise, amaz'd, temp'rate and furious,
Loyal and neutral in a moment? No man.

(Macbeth [II, 3])

The concept of insight in analysis has followed an odd trajectory. From its status as the means that achieved the analytic goal, it has become diluted by our realization that many other nonanalytic factors play a necessary role in a successful analysis (see Chapter 10). Since then, it has been degraded to the status of an isolated cognition, as in the phrase "merely intellectual insight." Clearly, this latter idea is based on a misunderstanding; one need consult no reference more modern than 1934, when back-to-back papers by Sterba (1934) and Strachey (1934) described the "mutative" event in analysis as one that combines affective (re)experiencing with reflective reconsideration.[1]

Although Macbeth points out that one does not experience cool reflection and heated passion in the same instant, the paired capacities to feel intensely and to step back and reflect are required of both members of the analytic couple.

In the next two chapters I will discuss the necessary complementarity of acting and reflecting – or participating and observing, or playing and critiquing – and try to point at the clinical problems when one or the other capacity is ineffective.

Note

1 For a thorough exploration of this point, and its relationship to working through, see Friedman (2019).

DOI: 10.4324/9781003360391-20

References

Friedman, L. (2019). *Freud's papers on technique and contemporary clinical practice.* Routledge.

Sterba, R. (1934). The fate of the ego in analytic therapy. *The International Journal of Psychoanalysis, 15*, 117–26.

Strachey, J. (1934). The nature of the therapeutic action of psycho-analysis. *The International Journal of Psychoanalysis,* 15, 127–59.

Chapter 16

In and Out of the Frame

Moving Between Experience and Reflection

Imagine being in a quiet room with sensory input strictly limited, so that cues to everyday social and material reality are minimized, and with motor activity restricted. These are the conditions for dreaming, for watching a movie, and for analysis. I would like to expand on these three frames and think a little about how they work, and what it means when they don't work. I will then suggest that one way to categorize the difficulties that certain patients encounter in the analytic situation is in terms of how they use adaptive regressive and self-observing capacities — in other words, how they characteristically deal with the framing of fantasy in analysis.

The audience at a movie exercises two complementary capacities: the ability to give oneself up to the action on the screen, to accept its premises, to let it be the whole world; and the ability to extricate oneself from the action on the screen, to re-enter the mundane world, and to think about the film from a perspective outside of it. In the context of movie-going, the first of these skills is sometimes called suspension of disbelief; the second is sometimes called critical thinking. A patient in analysis is called upon to use the same two complementary capacities. In analytic language, the first is sometimes called adaptive regression or "regression in service of the ego"; the second is called reflection, self-observing capacity, or "psychological-mindedness." The movies and analysis both establish the conditions for the exercise of these paired skills by exploiting what the philosopher Maurice Natanson (1962, p. 81) calls the "astonishing sorcery of the art apprentice" — the act of framing.

Putting a frame around something tells us to narrow the focus of our attention to what it contains and to suspend attention to everything else. It tells us to look in a different way — to consider the object out of its familiar role and context in terms of its form, its color, its relations exclusively within its bounded universe. It invites us to suspend disbelief in what it contains, if its contents conflict with everyday reality. And, by providing a plain line of demarcation between inside and outside, it makes it safe to surrender to its alternative universe by making it clear that we can come and go across that line. In other words, the observer is in a position to disavow the content of a

DOI: 10.4324/9781003360391-21

frame upon leaving it: "It's only a dream." I will come back to the significance of that disavowal later on.

A frame may be spatial – a picture frame, a playground, a stage, a screen – or temporal – a recess, a vacation, an analytic hour, a happy hour. It may be purely mental, as a daydream, or by social agreement, as in someone saying, "Look at that sunset!" or "Try to say everything that comes to mind."

As a brief illustration of problems with each of the paired abilities – adaptive regression and reflection – consider two stories. The first is the old joke in which a psychologist administers a Rorschach test. The subject describes each card in turn as portraying a sex act. When the psychologist says something about the patient's preoccupation with sex, he responds with, "Me? You're the one showing me all the dirty pictures!" The second is a story about Pablo Picasso, who found himself confronted by a man who took exception to the artist's portrayal of people. He complained that they didn't look like people. He then took a picture out of his wallet, saying, "This is what a real person looks like. This is my wife." Picasso looked at the photo and said, "I see. She's rather small. And flat."

In the Rorschach joke, the patient gave himself up to the imaginary – we might say he entered the frame of the inkblots. But then he could not extricate himself from it and reflect on what he saw as his own. From his perspective, his experience was ordinarily real. In the Picasso story, the man with the photo could not enter Picasso's framed world and accept its premises. Picasso responded in kind by refusing to enter the photographic frame, instead treating the photograph as ordinarily real. In each case, the distinction between what is real and what is imagined – the frame – is collapsed.

In what follows I would like to discuss three versions of one particular kind of frame[1] – dreaming, watching a movie, and analysis.

To begin with, dreams. Under conditions of motor inhibition and an absolute minimum of sensory input, the dreamer is freed from social and practical obligations, unable to act, unable to test the dream content against perceived reality. We might add as an aside, which we will return to when we consider dreams reported in analysis, that the dreamer has a claim to innocence due to the absence of conscious will. In that state, our minds are free to dream.

Freud (1900) said a dream was a disguised hallucinatory wish-fulfillment – that is to say, a dream is a compromise of wishes, prohibitions, and accommodations to reality that determines its final disguised form. In 1900 Freud's emphasis was on the wishful content, but consider what happens when the disguise fails. When a forbidden dream wish comes too close to availability to consciousness, it becomes a nightmare – and we *wake up*. In other words, we leave the frame, we leave the theatre of dreams in a hurry.

Note that what makes a dream into a nightmare is the too-close conformity of a dangerous fantasy to perception – a danger of the dream being too real. The motive for disguising a dream wish is the belief that getting one's wish would have dangerous consequences. So would knowing one's wish if, as in a dream, the distinction between thinking and acting is obliterated: the dream is lived as experience rather than as thought, and dreaming (or wishing) is experienced as acting.

We might note also that we have provided one definition of psychic trauma: When reality conforms too closely to fantasy, our omnipotence of thought may seem to be confirmed. Then our murderous thoughts make us feel as if we were murderers; our lustful thoughts make us feel as if we were seducers or rapists. That is one reason why victims of childhood sexual abuse have to insist on their absolute passivity when they recall the abusive situation; any hint of activity, excitement, or pleasure makes them feel as if they had been complicit in a sexual crime. These are instances in which the frame is not exited but broken: the boundary between fantasy and reality is erased, and life becomes a nightmare from which one is unable to awake.

Now, I would like to illustrate the impact of moving in and out of the fantasy frame by turning to two films. The first has as one of its themes the consequences of breaching a dreamlike frame, and the second tries to break its own frame for dramatic effect. As it happens, the first movie is a good one and the second is a bad one, but that is beside the point at the moment.

In Bertolucci's 1972 film *Last Tango in Paris*, starring Marlon Brando and Maria Schneider, a young woman has a chance encounter with a man in an empty apartment, which turns into an ongoing sexual affair. The two meet only in the apartment, and, at the man's insistence, no names or personal information are exchanged. The woman continues to have an ordinary life completely apart from the affair; in fact, she is planning to marry. Toward the end of the movie, the man changes the rules about the arrangement for reasons that need not concern us. He takes the woman out, and he tells her his name. He thinks things are better this way, but this is not his story; he is oblivious to the mounting tension that she and the audience feel. He follows her to her apartment, he playfully puts on her father's hat, and she finds a gun and kills him. The film ends with her rehearsing what she will say to the police: She doesn't know him; he followed her home and forced his way into the apartment.

In the idiom we are considering, the apartment they shared framed the affair, as distinct from her ordinary life as a dream from the waking state. When the frame was breached, the dream became a nightmare.[2] Killing her lover was a way to wake up; she then reframed the situation with a "secondary revision."[3]

The subject of the movie (at least for my thesis) is the blurring of the boundary between fantasy and reality, but the production itself is a frame that remains intact. In other words, the audience can enter the world on screen and then leave it again in a nonproblematic way. But now let us turn to a movie that takes liberties with the frame – the 1959 William Castle horror film *The Tingler*, starring Vincent Price. In this film a scientist has discovered a dangerous creature that feeds on fear but is paralyzed by screaming. The creature escapes, and the scientist trails it to a silent movie theatre. As we see Price throw the switch to bring up the house lights in the on-screen theatre, the house lights come up in our theatre as well. The screen is no longer visible, but Price's voice tells us the creature is loose and exhorts us to scream for our lives. A live actor planted in *our* theatre then rushes out with something in his arms, and Price tells us the creature has been subdued and we can return to our movie. As our houselights go down, we see Price in the act of throwing the switch again, and the movie continues.

Castle's mixed media production tries to play on the nightmare terror that is created when the frame between fantasy and reality is breached – suddenly the dream is encroaching on our waking life. But, as may be evident, it does not work, not only because it is so hokey but also because Castle misunderstood the way an audience watches a movie. As an audience, we do not identify with an audience – to do so would be a failure to enter into the frame. Rather, we give up our audience-selves and put ourselves in the action. Castle's trick pulled us out of it by making us aware of being an audience. In effect, he pushed us further away from our fantasy participation rather than including us in it; instead of losing ourselves in the movie, we become self-conscious, like unwilling participants at a sing-along.

There have been many successful instances of playing with the boundary between audience and actor – what theatre people call "breaking the fourth wall." Not all fail as spectacularly as *The Tingler*; the ones that succeed take note of the location of the audience's identification. But there is always a risk involved in breaking the mood. Freeman (2004) pointed out how intentional breaks in the theatrical frame follow a "trajectory of accommodation," from being rebellious to familiar to cliché. We might also think of it as a sequence of reframing that leads to ever tamer versions. The ultimate reframing of *The Tingler* was to make it a cult film like *The Rocky Horror Picture Show*, in which the audience took Castle's expanded frame and included it in an even larger frame with the audience shouting out the lines. It still has a frame (it is an "event"), but what was meant to be frightening became awkward and then became kitsch.

At this point, I would like to consider analysis and some of its frames and frames-within-frames. Although the goal of analysis is to clarify reality and distinguish it from fantasy, the means to that end require maximal access to fantasy. The analytic situation is set up with that in mind: the analyst is out of sight; the patient is physically comfortable, but action is restricted; the lighting is subdued; and the patient is encouraged to say everything. The situation is further constructed to be consistent and predictable, with clear starting and ending points, a tacit understanding that the analytic action stays in the office, and a promise from the analyst to put the patient's experience at center stage. The patient is told that there will be no social consequence of what she might say. Privacy, including confidentiality, is guaranteed.

These conditions are what "frame theorists" refer to as *the* frame, within which we are considering another frame. The arrangements approach those for dreaming, and the patient is being asked to let herself daydream. They also call to mind the situation of sitting in a darkened theatre – with the important difference being that the dreamer/patient is also the playwright. The freedom to daydream is directly related to the sense that it is safe to give oneself up to one's imagination within the relatively clear limits of the analytic situation – to "regress" to a state of play, to create the text of analysis so that subsequently one can reflect on it.[4]

Everyone has some trouble with either or both of the abilities involved in the back-and-forth dialogue between imagining and testing reality. All of us need to cling to the real at times; all of us need to disavow it at times. Often we split the difference: the hysteric who says "I know this isn't the case, but I really feel ..." treats the feeling as real despite judging it to be otherwise; the obsessional who says "It could be this way or that way" tells himself that what he feels to be true does not count, so he needn't notice that his preference is based on fantasy. If we play with the word "real," we might think of psychopathology as reification – treating something imaginary as real – and insight as realization – recognizing a fantasy conviction to be unrealistic.

But what we imprecisely call "analyzability" in some measure depends on the *potential* to recognize the two realms as separate. Generally, we do not try to analyze delusional patients, who have obliterated the frame around fantasy and live it as real. Similarly, the patient who desperately needs to shut down her imagination (or misattribute it) does not have a great prognosis in analytic treatment. The Rorschach subject's "dirty pictures" are not available as data about the subject, at least not at the time. These conditions may change; a good deal of work that is sometimes described as "preanalytic therapy" helps the patient access either the capacity to imagine or the capacity to reflect in order to make further analytic work possible.

Let us consider what these capacities and their associated problems look like in the analytic situation. One patient began his analysis by lying down on the couch and complaining about how uncomfortable it was. He then complained about how cold the office was. After the patient listed several more discomforts, the analyst ventured the suggestion that the patient was saying he was uncomfortable about being in the analytic situation. The patient explained with some irritation that he was not speaking in metaphors; the couch *was* uncomfortable, the room *was* cold, and it didn't mean anything else (he might have added, "Sometimes a cigar is just a cigar"). It soon became clear that the patient was not about to entertain the idea that he might imagine anything; imagining, to him, was the same as being wrong, which was the same as being crazy. He needed always to feel certain about what was real.

Another man, reluctantly accepting his male analyst's invitation to lie on the couch, promptly began to panic. He thought the analyst was getting out of his chair and reaching for him. He felt as if the room were spinning. The analyst had him sit up after about five excruciating minutes, by which time it had become clear to both of them that the patient could not tolerate the arrangement. The patient was aware that he was imagining things (at least in retrospect), but he could not exit the fantasy he was caught up in to consider it in any useful way. The treatment continued face to face.

As may be evident, the distinction between the two capacities of self-observation and adaptive regression maps onto the distinction between observing and participating. We ask our patients to be participant-observers of their own life narratives in the analytic situation. The analyst is, of course, also a participant/observer and requires the same paired capacities. If they cannot "participate," i.e., give themselves up to the experience, they will be critics with nothing to review. If they cannot observe themselves, they will be actors without an audience.

We might also divide those who privilege one capacity over the other into those who live out affect at the expense of reflection and those who use self-observation to avoid affect. In the theatre of affect, the hysteric is a player and the obsessional is a critic, but neither ever sees the play. Of course, people do not divide up so extremely. Most of the people we end up seeing have enough of each capacity to participate in an analytic treatment.

A particularly vexing version of the failure to use these capacities to complement each other arises for some nonpsychotic patients whose problematic adaptation to life involves the pervasive use of disavowal – what I called the "perverse attitude toward reality" in Chapter 4. These patients seem able to tell the difference between the real and the imaginary, yet in the face of anxiety they obliterate that frame and either treat reality as if it were an illusion or treat fantasies as if they were real. Calef (1972) gave a beautiful example of the latter case when he described a patient who complained chronically of insomnia, yet he never seemed to suffer from lack of sleep. An occasion arose by accident that revealed that the patient had been dreaming that he was awake. He never questioned the dream experience, i.e., he never applied his reflective, self-observing capacity to the lived dream.

As to the former case – treating reality as if it were an illusion – remember this example from Chapter 5:

A man in analysis was complaining about his wife, who had noticed an ominous-looking mole on his arm and suggested he see a doctor. He was annoyed with her worrying him and being unsupportive. He had not gone to the doctor. It soon became clear that he had noticed the mole also but had shrugged it off by telling himself it had *probably* always been there. He wanted to talk about what in his past had made him so prone to bodily worries. I commented on him saying the mole had "probably" always been there; had it, or hadn't it? When he let himself think about it, he realized he had noticed it had changed in size and appearance recently;

in fact, that was what had prompted his wife's remark. Now he was anxious and said, "I have the fantasy I have cancer." He wondered why he got caught up in such fantasies and wanted to explore that propensity.

I said that what was troubling him was not the fantasy but the reality of his changing mole, which he wanted desperately to discount by telling himself it was a fantasy. He recognized this trait in himself and connected it to similar instances of disavowal we had discussed before. He wanted to pursue the psychological meaning of it as we had done in the past – for example, about whether something he had experienced had been a dream or a reality. He considered some genetic antecedents. I told him I thought he was calming himself by making the terrifying reality of the mole into a psychological issue. Again, he recognized his tendency and wanted to explore this interesting hypothesis. As the hour was ending, I said we had much to understand but no amount of exploration was going to make the mole less dangerous.

With this sort of patient, the analyst's role of speaking for reality even while trying to analyze the patient's efforts to discount it may have to be much greater than with a neurotic patient – not to protect the patient from psychotic regression but to help him stop bumping into the furniture of disavowed reality. This includes the treatment reality: These patients may treat the entire work of analysis with what the first President Bush called "plausible deniability." In and out of analysis, they obliterate the frame between reality and illusion and come down firmly on neither side.

For many patients, and for these patients especially, the termination phase is crucial. It is the time when patients who have learned to talk the analytic talk will find out if they can walk the analytic walk. It is the time when apparent insight may be revealed to be compliance in service of an unanalyzed fantasy dependent on the analyst's presence. In a paper on termination, Loewald (1988) noted the paradox of trying to analyze while dismantling the analytic machinery. We might say that during termination the timeless dreamlike frame is dismantled, the patient is obligated to wake up and live in real time, and only then can the two parties see clearly what the patient will be able to take away from the analytic stage and carry into her daily life.

I would like to end this chapter with a slight digression to fulfill my earlier promise and pursue a few thoughts about dreams in analysis, in the context of the sorcery of frames. The utility of dreams in analysis extends beyond the fact that the conditions for dreaming produce less-disguised primary process material. I would like to make two observations about dreams as reported in analysis, which will be familiar to all analysts. First, by virtue of being framed as a dream, the patient feels a certain freedom to report material that would otherwise be intolerable. It is precisely the built-in disavowal provided by the frame – "It's only a dream" – that makes it available to conscious awareness.

Curiously, the second feature that makes dreams so useful in analysis is that, despite the disavowal of responsibility, there can be no question about the authorship of a dream. This is a very useful combination of traits that is very economically illustrated by a story from Poland's (1996) chapter "The analyst's words." He told about a woman in analysis who said of her dream, "I would never do anything so outrageous as what the dream suggests." To which he replied, "You wouldn't even dream of such a thing" (p. 104).

Freud (1900) made the observation that many dreams express the effort to disavow a wish by claiming it is only a dream (pp. 338, 488–9). Dreams within the frame of analysis always have that potential. It seems to me that these two traits of dreams – the disavowability of their significance and their unambiguous authorship – allow the exercise of the two capacities we have been discussing: the analysand can use the disclaimer of disavowability to allow herself to enter into the frame of the dream and imagine, and she can also use the disclaimer to extricate herself and reflect on the dream as a self-created object. These two complementary capacities, for adaptive regression and for self-observation, are the foundation upon which both analytic work and art appreciation are based. It is the sorcery of frames, whether analytic or artistic, that facilitates the adaptive movement between surrendering to fantasy and applying judgment.

Notes

1 I am aware that there is a considerable literature about "the" analytic frame, which some analysts refer to as "frame theory." This is not a contribution to that body of thought; I intend my usage of the word to be common English.
2 Mark Scott (personal communication, 2004) pointed out that the dream wish was an affair with her father, which forced its way to consciousness via the hat.
3 That Bertolucci was aware of how films frame illusion from reality might be adduced from the character of the woman's fiancé, a young filmmaker who walks through life making imaginary film frames with his fingers. The casting is also relevant: the role is played by the filmmaker François Truffaut.
4 Louis Roussel (personal communication) raised a cogent question: What really happens when we "step back" to reflect? He argued that we cannot actually extricate ourselves from our experience as if we had transcended it. I think "stepping back" is shorthand for shifting from the experiential context to a larger context that includes it, along with the judgment we apply to it (see Bateson, 1972). I also believe that the shift to a more inclusive context changes the experience as it is remembered. This is a fair definition of insight.

References

Bateson, G. (1972). *Steps to an ecology of mind*. Jason Aronson.

Calef, V. (1972). "I am awake": Insomnia or dream? An addendum to the forgetting of dreams. *The Psychoanalytic Quarterly, 41*(2), 161–71.

Freeman, P.S. (2004, March 19). *The over-luxuriant fantasy* [Paper presentation]. Intersession of the San Francisco Psychoanalytic Institute, San Francisco.

Freud, S. (1900). The interpretation of dreams. *SE 4–5.*

Loewald, H.W. (1988). Termination analyzable and unanalyzable. *The Psychoanalytic Study of the Child, 43*, 155–66.

Natanson, M.A. (1962). *Literature, philosophy, and the social sciences: Essays in existentialism and phenomenology.* Martinus Nijhoff.

Poland, W.S. (1996). *Melting the darkness. The dyad and principles of clinical practice.* Jason Aronson.

Chapter 17

Play in Analysis[1]

In this chapter I would like to talk about the patient's and the analyst's capacities to play, and to forgo play for reality. My thesis, as introduced in the previous chapter, is that in order to get the most out of play (or out of watching a play), you have to be able to do two things: give yourself up to the experience, then take some distance to review the play.

Freud (1908) wrote, "The opposite of play is not what is serious but what is real" (p. 143). Analytic work requires *both* participants to be able to move from one position to the other – to immerse themselves in the action or give themselves up to fantasy, then to step out of it in order to look at it from the outside, with fresh eyes. To use Freud's distinction, to move between the play and the real.

Most patients (and probably most analysts) are better at one capacity than the other. By way of illustration, recall the joke about the Rorschach test from the previous chapter. The punchline was "You're the one showing me the dirty pictures!"

Now consider a variation: Another Rorschach subject describes each card as a piece of cardboard with ink on it. The first Rorschach subject enters into play but cannot step out to think about it; the second cannot let his imagination go to play with the card and accept it on its own terms. The first is an uncritical player; the second is a critic who cannot play.

Although the bulk of Freud's writing put the emphasis on the reflective, interpretive position of the analyst, he does give us hints about the analyst's "playing with," e.g., when he talks about the analyst's unconscious as a receiver turned to the patient's unconscious; and, if we hunt, we can find a few examples of the analyst's "playing out" a role with the patient. In the second hour of the analysis of Lieutenant Lorenz, the "Rat Man," the patient recalls the "rat torture" that gives the case its nickname. Freud reports:

> Here the patient broke off, got up from the sofa, and begged me to spare him the recital of the details. *I assured him that I myself had no taste whatever*

DOI: 10.4324/9781003336039I-22

for cruelty, and certainly had no desire to torment him, but that naturally
I could not grant him something which was beyond my power.

                            (Freud, 1909, p. 165; italics added)

At the end of this second session the patient behaved as though he were
dazed and bewildered. He repeatedly addressed me as "Captain," probably *because* at the beginning of the hour I had told him that I myself
was not fond of cruelty like Captain N, and that I had no intention of
tormenting him unnecessarily.

                            (Freud, 1909, p. 169; italics added)

Note the "because": I imagine what happened was that, after he saw the
patient's reaction, Freud retrospectively heard his own negation – "*I assured
him that I myself had no taste whatever for cruelty*" – and discovered he had been
playing a role that he will ultimately interpret as a father transference.

I would now like to turn to two clinical presentations by James M. Herzog.
In the first (2011a), he described the play in the analyst's mind, and in fact
his paper is an *example* of the analyst at play. He is not suggesting that this is
some technical innovation, but rather that this is what we all do, all the time,
and it merits our attention.

It is an irony of our field that it took so long for us to get around to thinking
about the fact that the analyst's psychology makes a material difference in the
course of analysis. Until fairly recently we have let stand the fiction that there
is an interchangeable "technique" we should strive to obtain, as if to erase the
analyst from the process. Herzog shows us the analyst's associations – that
is, we see him *daydreaming*. The analyst's daydreams determine, among other
things, what merits commentary; in other words, the *interface* between the
patient's actions and the analyst's daydreams defines the so-called "analytic
surface" and the so-called "point of affective urgency."

But in his clinical examples, Herzog also demonstrates the role of play in
the other sense, in which play is identified with *action* as distinguished from
reflection – "playing out" rather than playing with. For instance, let us look at
the situation with his patient Margarita, a 41-year-old married physician who
had begun to realize that her father had been sexually involved with another
man since she was a little girl. Margarita seemed to be working well in analysis, and I got the impression that she made no waves. Then a year into the
work, she sent Herzog a video, with an email request that he view it before
the next hour. Herzog described his reaction in detail, including the "technical dilemma" in which he was placed, and the fantasy that there was a virus
in the email.

Herzog wondered: What kind of play is this? The answer is not simple.
If we consider what Margarita did – researching the analyst as she had her

father, contacting him outside the office, making a demand on his free time, and so on – it starts to look less like play and more like an effort to *reify* something, to make the relationship with Herzog into something real beyond the confines of the analytic playroom. This forced Herzog into a choice of actions; he settled for what he called a "compromise" by emailing her back to suggest they talk about it in the office.

What Herzog subsequently did with this incident (and which he began in his email) was to reframe the action in which the two of them are engaged as play available for commentary. Together they followed a line of inquiry – even as other scenarios are played out without reflection. I want to emphasize that *this is not a comment on Herzog's clinical decision*, which I have largely omitted as irrelevant to my purposes. In my view it is a fact of analytic life that, even as you work interpretively on one thing, you play out others in unexamined action.

To continue the illustration, here is Margarita's response in the session after the email exchange: "How utterly unanalytic of me to do that. How totally analytic of you that you responded with your email." Herzog ponders one meaning of that, the idealization of him and denigration of herself, and we don't know what other meanings they may have considered subsequently. The one that smacked me in the face was why a patient should judge herself on a scale of being analytic. Being analytic is an idealization only if being an analyst is the ideal. Here I have the impression that the two of them are engaged in an unexamined play about being analytic (and about role reversibility) even as they analyze the play about the emails to learn about the gender-bending relationship to her father.

By the endpoint of this report, Herzog knows a good deal about the patient's inner world (which is to say, about her version of the "outer world"): in Margarita's world the email incident represented her (partly successful) effort to seduce the analyst. In the analytic commentary on what was played out, the patient says that, unlike her father, the analyst is "a man whom a little girl could seduce, who would love her in return, even though she should never have seduced him in the first place." The analyst seems to accept that "narrative," as Herzog calls it.

But consider that quote. It implies that her father did not love her and that she could not seduce him, presumably *because he preferred males*. Further, she says she should never have seduced him in the first place. Since when is it the child's job to refrain from seducing the parent? Creating the narrative – making sense of the play – is the analyzing function; accepting the patient's narrative is reentering the play. The thought about seducing the analyst is also played out – enacted in the transference – in her criticizing herself for being "unanalytic": since when is it the patient's job to be analytic? Is she demonstrating an unconscious belief that the analyst wants her to be more like him?

I have already contended that it is an unavoidable consequence of the nature of human interaction that, even as they are analyzing one region of the play space, they are playing in another. Herzog refers to her discovery of her father's secret life as "abandonment." How is it that? We didn't hear anything to suggest that he stopped being her father when he had his affair; he was no more married to her before than after. Another possibility (in my associative play again) is that she and the analyst are playing out a scenario in which she maintains the conviction that she *could* have seduced her father away from her mother, if only he hadn't had something "wrong" with him.

Both analyst and patient seem to accept what seems to me an unlikely premise as a fact: that her father had no interest in her because he didn't like girls.[2] This is a neighborhood in Margarita's world in which the play goes on, and which (as far as we know) has not been made the subject of analytic commentary.

If we think of the analytic process as a series of enacted scenes followed by commentary from the two reviewers' perspective, a complication immediately comes to mind (I mean a complication in the work, not in the theory): As I have just suggested, while one is commenting on the play, one is also acting in another play. The complication comes up when the play is playing at doing analysis. This is an especially common and thorny difficulty with adults in treatment: How do you distinguish genuine analytic collaboration from compliance in service of a hidden transference wish? Herzog gives an example of when Margarita tried to recast the email incident as a matter of her being unanalytic. Because of the word "analytic," it would have been easy to miss; being "analytic" sounds like something we want our patients to aspire to, if we don't think about it too hard (in contrast, imagine if she had said, "How completely male of you ... how completely female of me"). But often the task is even harder; sometimes we don't catch on until termination becomes an issue that the patient has learned to talk the analytic talk but not to walk the analytic walk.

This is why, although I don't treat children, I try to hear as many child analytic case presentations as possible. With adults one may be lulled by the compliance with language into missing the action. Children don't let you get away with that. To borrow a phrase from chess, they get you out of the books and make you think freshly about what you are trying to do. In the other Herzog contribution (2011b), nine-year-old Ezra began his first session by sweeping all the books off the analyst's shelf. Neither he nor Brad (see below) is about to fool us with his compliance by learning the analyst's language.

With the seven-year-old Brad (Herzog, 2011a) we have a different problem. Brad doesn't make eye contact; he either keeps his mouth shut or pours out neologisms that Herzog says were directed outward but not to him. In other words, he keeps all his bodily doors and windows closed to other people. But he pushes a screwdriver into his arm as he thinks of his parents, and he says Herzog looks like a penis. Herzog's associations to the screwing were to the active position: "Brad likes to cut ... [or to] play at cutting." Mine were to the passive position. I heard "You look like a penis" as "Are you going to penetrate me?" Brad is pursued by Klingons and he speaks Klingon, but I don't know if he ever gets that he is the Klingons.

Is Brad playing with the analyst? Actually, I don't think so. Herzog makes the point that a defining feature of play is its reversibility. I agree with that statement completely: If you can't leave the stage or the playground, there is no play. In other words, the reversibility that matters is the capacity to move between play and reality.

Consider the Rorschach joke: The subject seems to be playing within the boundaries of the cards when he describes the dirty pictures. But then he reveals that he cannot exit the play and review it – it is not reversible, and so it is not available to enlighten the subject. If the distinction is obliterated, then what looks like play is simply the patient's reality.

Notes

1 A version of this chapter was originally presented at the Scientific Meeting of the San Francisco Psychoanalytic Society, December 12, 2011.
2 My experience with patients of either sex is that when a parent's affair is discovered by a child, the child tends to take it as confirmation that the parent *is* seducible – but not by the child.

References

Freud, S. (1908). Creative writers and day-dreaming. SE *10*, 141–54.
Freud, S. (1909). Notes upon a case of obsessional neurosis. SE *10*, 151–310.
Herzog, J.M. (2011a, December 12). *Play in adult and child analysis: The concept of countertransference play* [Paper presentation]. San Francisco Psychoanalytic Society.
Herzog, J.M. (2011b, December 10). *Unpublished case report* [Case report presentation]. San Francisco Psychoanalytic Institute Candidates' Colloquium.

Coda

Writing About Analytic Writing

The ability to write clearly about analysis does not come with the license to practice. Some analysts are gifted writers – Jay Greenberg, Ted Jacobs, Thomas Ogden, and Warren Poland immediately come to mind – and some hack through a thicket of linguistic brambles to deliver their ideas to their analytic colleagues.

Unfortunately, much of the analytic literature is barely readable, and not because the ideas are difficult (which they are). Many brilliant analysts think idiosyncratically, and some of them won't (or can't) take the trouble to translate their thoughts into the common tongue. Other analysts, not so gifted, use analytic jargon to paper over the cracks in their thinking.

As a teacher I am repeatedly impressed by the reverence candidates in training have for the most incomprehensible analytic writers. I have already voiced my suspicion that the beginner's anxiety about the difficulty of clinical work is often displaced onto the complexity of the theory – after all, even the most perplexing theory can be mastered eventually. In some analytic discussions, incoherence is taken for inscrutable wisdom.

In this coda I reveal my attitude toward the state of analytic writing in decreasingly kosher ways. Chapter 18 is a straightforward critique of Winnicott's (to me) unnecessarily difficult theoretical writing and of Ogden's appreciation of it. Chapter 19 is a brief satire of what might be called analysis misappropriated. Chapter 20 is a spoof of a modern analytic paper, which I guarantee is funnier than *Oedipus Rex*.

The comedian Steven Wright once said that he wished that his first spoken word had been "Quote." Then, on his deathbed, he could have said "Unquote." My first contribution to the analytic literature (1981) was a limerick, so I am especially chuffed to end this offering with a satire.

Reference

Grossman, L.P. (1981). L.P. Grossman on projective identification. Letter to the editor. *International Review of Psychoanalysis, 8*, 342.

DOI: 10.4324/9781003360391-23

Chapter 18

Reading Ogden Reading Winnicott

I have always enjoyed reading Winnicott's clinical work. His writing is playful, startling, provocative, often elegant, and always lively. His papers are frequently cited – perhaps even more often than they are read. In the opinion of Thomas Ogden (2001), psychoanalysis has had "only one great English speaking writer" (p. 299), Winnicott – an accolade for which Ogden himself might be in contention.

Yet for all his liveliness and originality, when I have been called upon to teach Winnicott's theoretical work, I have come up against two problems: First, I found that frequently I could not say what he meant, especially whether he meant to be taken metaphorically or literally. His use of words, including psychoanalytic terms, is often idiosyncratic and rarely elaborated. Second, I found in many cases that I could not tell how he arrived at his conclusions. He is apt to state an idea as a fact almost in passing; he does not usually explain, or even acknowledge, that others might have other ideas. When I turned to Ogden for help, I found both enlightenment and further confusion.

In what follows I would like to share my reading of Ogden's paper "Reading Winnicott" (2001). I will try to show that Winnicott's writing style, enjoyable though it may be, does not encourage the reader to engage in dialogue with his ideas. After doing so, I would like to respond to what I believe is a false dichotomy set up by Ogden between those analysts who embrace "the indissoluble interpenetration of life and art" and those who despair that "the discourse among analysts ... will forever remain limited by our imprecise, impressionistic – and consequently confusing and misleading – accounts of what we observe and how we think about what we do as analysts" (Ogden, 2001, p. 321).

Ogden's paper is a reading of the paper "Primitive Emotional Development" (Winnicott, 1945), which he identifies as Winnicott's earliest major contribution. Ogden shows admirably how Winnicott's writing style evokes, rather than simply describes, the ideas he is trying to convey. He compares the writing to poetry, especially to Frost and Borges, for the compactness and richness of the language. But he also insists from the first page that "what

DOI: 10.4324/9781003360391-24

'Primitive Emotional Development' has to offer to a psychoanalytic reader *cannot be said in any other way* (which is to say that the writing is extraordinarily resistant to paraphrase)" (Ogden, 2001, p. 299; italics added, parentheses in original).

I find this conclusion very troubling. To say something "cannot be said in any other way" is to say that there can be no answer to the question: What do you mean? If it is true that it cannot be paraphrased, we are left with something far worse than "imprecision." The implication is that we cannot agree on what Winnicott is saying even to evaluate it critically. This is not the case with poetry and certainly not with Borges[1] or Frost; with their works, we immerse ourselves in them, we let them affect us – and then we step back and use our critical thinking. I cannot think of a Borges story or Frost poem that left me confused as to what the author meant to the extent that I could not agree on the meaning with others. I can say what they mean. My paraphrase may be bad poetry, but then I don't expect poetry to articulate psychoanalytic theory. Ambiguous, paradoxical, or contradictory ideas do not require ambiguous, paradoxical, or contradictory descriptions; to the contrary, one of the tasks of psychoanalytic writing is to expose and clarify the nature of the paradoxes or contradictions that cannot be resolved.

In any case, it seems that Ogden does not believe his own assertion. In his first example, in which Winnicott describes how his own mind works, Ogden unpacks Winnicott's paragraph in one slightly longer paragraph (Ogden, 2001, p. 392). Apparently it can be done, after all; Ogden does so throughout the paper.

In some instances, Ogden argues that (presumably as with poetry) the reader has to "do the work" to glean the meaning. In his second example, Winnicott describes the depressed patient, about which Ogden writes:

> In the space of a single sentence, Winnicott suggests (by means of his *use of the idea*, rather than through his explication of it) that depression is a manifestation of the patient's taking on as his own, (in fantasy, taking into himself) the mother's depression ... with the unconscious aim of relieving her of her depression. What is astounding is that this conception of the patient's depression is presented not through a direct statement, but by means of a sentence that is virtually incomprehensible unless the reader takes the initiative of doing the work of creating/discovering the conception of the intergenerational origins and dynamic structure of depression.
>
> (Ogden, 2001, p. 303; italics in original)

Ogden points out that this is a theory of depression that is radically different from those of Freud and Klein. Thankfully, Ogden paraphrased Winnicott's sentences to make them clear, even to me, without my having to "take the initiative of doing the work of creating/discovering." Ogden made it plain, and he made it possible for me to consider whether Winnicott's position fits my own clinical experience. Why didn't Winnicott do that? Ogden tells us that Winnicott "demands that the reader become an active partner in the creation of meaning" (2001, p. 305). Yet Winnicott seems pretty certain of his own meaning; he just seems reluctant to spell it out. He appears to take for granted the correctness of his theory of depression and does not feel any responsibility for defending it – or even elaborating it.

A little further on Ogden credits a passage from Winnicott with "a major revision of psychoanalytic technique. He accomplishes this so subtly that the reader is apt not to notice it .... Nothing short of a new way of being with and talking to patients is being offered to the reader, without preaching or fanfare" (Ogden, 2001, pp. 307–8).

Without fanfare indeed: the reader is apt not to notice it. How did that become a virtue of psychoanalytic writing? How did "virtually incomprehensible" psychoanalytic theorizing become admirable?[2] To me, Winnicott's style discourages, rather than invites, a dialogue with his ideas.

At one point Ogden apologizes for his awkward language (2001, p. 305, footnote), but I, for one, am grateful; I find Ogden far more understandable than Winnicott. There are times when Ogden's exegesis does not convince me, but I am not left trying to figure out what he meant. I find I can engage with Ogden's Winnicott more readily than with Winnicott.

Ogden is exceptionally generous. For example, he quotes a sentence from Winnicott that begins, "Once dreams are remembered and even conveyed somehow to a third person." He admits that he finds the sentence "jarring and confusing" (Ogden, 2001, p. 312), but after some gymnastics he concludes that, thanks to Winnicott, "the reader experiences what it feels like for a child to be two people and not to notice that experience until an adult gives him help in 'getting to know ... [what are becoming *his*] dreams'" (p. 312; parentheses and italics in original).

This reader did not have that experience. And after hearing Ogden's imaginative reading, I know something about Ogden's thinking but not much about Winnicott's. I don't read psychoanalytic theory in order to "experience what it feels like" to be an infant, because I don't take it on faith that any analyst knows what that feels like.[3] I read in order to find out what the author thinks might be the case and why he thinks so. Winnicott does not often tell us how he came to his conclusions.

For another example, Ogden (2001, p. 305) notes Winnicott's revolutionary reconception of the analytic frame implicit in the following citation: "the end of the hour, the end of the analysis, the rules and regulations, these all come as expressions of [the analyst's] hate" (Winnicott, 1945, p. 147). But other than adding that "this theme could be developed extensively and usefully," there is no further discussion from Winnicott, no hint of awareness that anyone might disagree or fail to understand, no suggestion that there might be other meanings. The idea is left to stand as if it were a simple fact.

Ogden's emphasis on the stimulating nature of Winnicott's writing seems one-sided to me. After a particularly charming quotation about what is going on in an infant's mind, Ogden writes:

> The reader of the sentence being discussed is not moved to question how Winnicott can possibly know what an infant feels, or to point out that regressions in the analyses of children and adults (whether psychotic, depressed, or quite healthy) bear a very uncertain correlation with infantile experience. Rather, the reader is inclined to suspend disbelief *for a time*, and to enter into the experience of reading (with Winnicott), allowing himself to be carried by the music of the language and ideas.
>
> (Ogden, 2001, p. 309; italics added, parentheses in original)

The phrase "for a time" points us to the neglected other half of Winnicott's writing. I agree with Ogden that participation in psychoanalytic reading, as in art, requires an immersion, a suspension of disbelief, a participation in the action – *for a time.* But it also requires a step back, a reflective act, an act of "psychological-mindedness" and critical thinking. If the reader is still "not moved to question," the author has failed at his task. One of those points that Ogden says we are not moved to question, the uncertain correlation between analytic regression and infantile experience, is fundamental to Winnicott's paper. He says on the first page, "Primarily interested in the child patient, and the infant, I decided that I must study psychosis in analysis" (1945, p. 145). He says nothing further about that decision. Winnicott was not moved to question that correlation either.

Artists may leave the critical thinking to the audience, but expository writers have an obligation to present an illustration or an argument, not merely a conclusion. When they do not, we are entitled to ask: How would you know if you were wrong? In the paragraph Ogden cited about how Winnicott's mind works, Winnicott writes, "What happens is that I gather this and that, here and there, settle down to clinical experience, form my own theories and then, last of all, interest myself in looking to see where I stole what" (1945, p. 392). He goes on to say to his audience at the British Psychoanalytical Society, "By listening to what I have to say, and criticizing, you help me to take my next step, which is to study the sources of my ideas, both in clinical work and in the published writings of analysts" (Winnicott, 1945, pp. 145–6). This is, as he just said, the *last* step. Did he skip the step in which the author considers the criticisms of others in order to further develop, modify, or correct his own ideas?

I would like to close by returning to Ogden's dichotomy. The division between analysts is not between the artists and the scientists or between those who privilege "impressionism" and those who privilege reason; it is between those who settle for one without the other and those who recognize the dialectical movement between them. The work of an analyst, of a patient, or of an artist's audience requires immersion in experience, complete with "suspension of disbelief" – *for a time*. Then it also requires distance, reflection, judgment, and critical thinking. Reflection without experience is empty; experience without reflection is blind.

Notes

1 Ogden cites a volume of Borges that has been translated from the original Spanish. Is translation not a form of paraphrase?
2 One well-known contributor to our literature once said without a trace of irony, "I'm such a good writer, people think they understand me when they don't."
3 I might read Winnicott's (1980) *The Piggle* for that purpose – but there the child speaks for herself.

References

Ogden, T.H. (2001). Reading Winnicott. *The Psychoanalytic Quarterly*, 70(2), 299–323.
Winnicott, D.W. (1945). *Through Paediatrics to Psychoanalysis*. Basic Books (1958).
Winnicott, D.W. (1980). *The Piggle*. The International Psycho-Analytical Library, 107, 1–201. The Hogarth Press and the Institute of Psycho-Analysis.

Chapter 19

The Duration of Analysis
A Contribution to the Discussion

A report by Renik (2001) described a psychoanalytic treatment that was completed in one 50-minute session. This tendency toward longer and longer analyses has prompted me to present the following case.

The Analysis

Mr. Schreber (not his real name) came to my office in the psychiatry clinic where I was a resident. Before I said anything, he began to speak: "I don't like psychiatrists. They're in their heads too much. Plus they think everyone else is crazy, when it's them that's crazy." He went on for another two minutes or so, listing the failures and abuses of psychiatrists. I then said, "With so many reasons not to come, I wonder why you came." He responded, "Good question. I'm outta here." He then got up and walked out.

Discussion

Initial Phase: Resistance to the Awareness of the Transference

Mr. Schreber came in with misgivings about me that became increasingly negative as he elaborated them. He took these preconceptions as simply real. This phase of the treatment lasted for 2 minutes, 30 seconds.

Middle Phase: Transference Neurosis

The material shifted when I intervened, opening the way for him to consider the presence of other feelings toward me. He put his newly discovered respect and affection for me eloquently: "Good question." This phase lasted for just under 2 seconds.

Termination Phase: Accepting Reality

After the affective breakthrough of the middle phase, Mr. Schreber began to think of reentering the flow of his life, much as Hans Castorp, the hero

DOI: 10.4324/9781003360391-25

of Thomas Mann's (1965) *Magic Mountain*, felt when he elected to leave the mountain and return to his life. He recognized the limitations of treatment and took decisive responsibility for his life as he announced, "I'm outta here." I believe we were both fittingly proud and a little sad to see our work wind down to its inevitable conclusion as he walked out the door. The termination phase lasted 12 seconds, counting the door closing.

Implications for Technique

The duration of Mr. Schreber's analysis was 2 minutes, 44 seconds (rounding up to the nearest second). In an era of analyses routinely dragging on for 10, 20, or (in Renik's case) even 50 minutes, it is certainly time we reconsidered some of the technical principles that continue to slow our work down.

In my view, primary among them is the outmoded insistence on the analyst waiting to speak until he understands something or has a question. In my example, I believe I could have shortened the treatment considerably had I just met Mr. Schreber at the door and told him to get a grip on himself. Attendance is another time sink; many interpretations are so generally applicable that they could be sent to the patient in advance of meeting, e.g., "You must feel the same way about me," or "You're trying to destroy the analysis" (the choice of interpretation depends, of course, on the analyst's theoretical orientation). Even if paring the length of analysis down to zero is an unattainable ideal, we can still go a lot further toward the fundamental analytic goal of getting patients out of our sight as fast as possible.

Postscript

Much like Freud (1909) in his addendum to the "Rat Man" case about the patient being cut down in the prime of life after his successful analysis, I am saddened to report this follow-up. Upon leaving my office, Mr. Schreber chanced to see a police officer who thought that my patient was homosexual. Mr. Schreber confronted the officer, hitting him from behind with a sourdough baguette, and was promptly arrested. It is tragic that, so soon after achieving his freedom from neurotic suffering, he should have had the misfortune to encounter someone so cruel as to transmit his accusatory thoughts telepathically.

References

Freud, S. (1909). Notes upon a case of obsessional neurosis. SE *10*, 151–318.
Mann, T. (1965). *The magic mountain* (H.T. Lowe-Porter, Trans.). Knopf.
Renik, O. (2001). The patient's experience of therapeutic benefit. *The Psychoanalytic Quarterly, 70*(1), 231–42.

Chapter 20

A Desultory Excursion into New Developments in Psychoanalysis

Since the early days of psychoanalysis, considerable emphasis has been placed on the endomorphic transfigurations from apathy to apostasy. For example, Sachertorte (1932) pointed out the tendency among bipeds toward the orotund and the profound while muttering in the mundane. Although there were a few dissenters (notably Grumbling, 1936, who objected that apostasy followed from ecstasy, and ecstasy was an escape from instasy), most analysts accepted the basic premise that the way to a man's heart was through his stomach, and the way through his stomach was alimentary.

In the postwar years, alimentary schools cropped up all over Europe and the United States, in the hope that enlightened child-rearing practices could replace and possibly prevent primitive child-fronting in the maximal adult; but alas, optimal and maximal are two different words (as are plump and dustbin, or thumb and butter). Despite the similarity of the optimal and the maximal, opticians thrived, while maxicians have all but disappeared.[1] It seems that, as is often the case, clinicians were ahead of theoreticians (by a neck, with administrators third by two lengths, and experimentalists bringing up the rear). Our theory has not yet caught up with our praxis when it comes to distinguishing the abstruse from the recondite.

Recently, though, a group of analysts adept in fuzzy logic has begun to update our theory and bring it into consonance with the Heisenberg uncertainty relation and the formulation of strange attractors in physics. So far they have succeeded in attracting the strangest of strangers and making our ideas fuzzier than a stuffed hedgehog and more uncertain than Jello. This advance could not have come about without the pioneering work of D.W. Pillicock (2011), Fogni Bologni (2020), and Mousse and Meringue (see, for example, 2021), whose ideas about fluffy logic took the remaining edge off our thinking. Lacque (2020), Stücke (2021), and Baral (2020) also contributed significantly with their ideas about left field theory and its applications.[2]

DOI: 10.4324/9781003360391-26

The Case of Frau Agnes

Perhaps no case of Freud's has stimulated less discussion than that of the "Hard of Hearing Woman," Frau Agnes (1894). Yet we still have much to learn from this case. Of all Freud's clinical reports, only the "Rat Man" paper (1909) includes any of Freud's actual notes, but only the analysis of Frau Agnes (1894) has an actual transcript of a session, thanks to the careful note taking of his next patient and the poor soundproofing of Freud's office. An excerpt from that session shows the limitations of Freud's work before the turn of the twentieth century:

PROF. DR. FREUD: Please continue, Frau Agnes.
FR. AGNES: What?
FREUD: I said continue.
AGNES: What?
FREUD: You seem to have trouble hearing.
AGNES: What? No, I don't like herring.

Discussion

As is apparent, Freud had no grasp of modern principles, although Jones (1972) has suggested that the Agnes case gave Freud the idea to feed the Rat Man herring to punish him for bringing up the rat torture. But today we have the tools to revisit this case and to explore the rich steaming load it has dropped in front of us. Consider, for instance, the first line of text: "Prof. Dr. FREUD." We know of course that Freud wasn't all uppercase; in fact, he was middlecase at best, reduced to seeing deaf patients who would not discern his middlecase accent. In fact, we may infer that Frau Agnes was also short-sighted, since she did not notice the "Prof." at the front of Freud's name – a distinction he would not earn for many years to come. Then note that Frau Agnes rejects the herring, even though Freud did not offer it. Clearly she perceived Freud as running a delicatessen.[3] This was the first recorded countertransference.

From these observations alone we can discern Freud's countercountertransference with a high degree of confidence unencumbered by evidence. It is apparent that Freud was caught up in an unexamined desire to make a living. The patient's difficulty hearing was thus a distortion in the service of protecting her true self from her false self and her multiple-choice selves. It represented a procedural memory of her problematic attachment expressed through the deli field shared by the co-conspirators. Who, after all, is the final arbiter of what is true? I am. Of course it is true that some of us are more egalitarian than others; yet it is vital that we continue translating our uncertainties into Latin and Greek, so that we can obscure our differences as we band together and overthrow the tyranny of the past in favor of the tyranny of the present.

Notes

1 Magicians are still with us, of course, along with maxipads and Mexico.
2 The thesis of Beebe (2000) was thrown out with de Bathvasser (1999).
3 Further evidence can be found in the "whitefish incident" (Freud, 1894, p. 64).

References

Baral, Craetan (2020). *Disturbances in the field* [Doctoral dissertation, University of Hard Knocks].

Beebe, Phoebe (2000). An elaboration *ad hominy* of de Bathvasser's good idea. *Yearbook of Informal Fallacies*, *23*, 111–232.

Bologni, F. (2020). La logica del tiramisu. *Ricerca sui Dolci, 14*, 92–113.

de Bathvasser, M. (1999). Eine gute idee. In Numpty (Ed.) *Geist und Scheisse*. Langweilig Verlag, 49–50.

de Bathvasser, M. (2001). Who asked you, anyway? A reply to P. Beebe. *Yearbook of Informal Fallacies*, *23*, 542.

Freud, S. (1894). Notes on a case of impaired hearing. SE *3*, 343–54.

Freud, S. (1909). Notes on a case of obsessional neurosis. SE *10*, 153–329.

Grumbling, Naomi (1936). Everything you know is wrong. *Journal of Unwarranted Conviction*, *1*, 1–11.

Jones, E. (1972). *Sigmund Freud: Life and work, v.1: The young Freud 1856–1900*. Hogarth Press.

Lacque, Jacques (2020). Outfield differentiation. In Tinker, Evers, & Chance (Eds.), *Inside Baseball*. Avarice & Cashin.

Mousse, C. & Meringue, L. (2021). Where are we, and who cares? *Journal of Psycholocation*, *16*, 3–213.

Pillicock, D.W. (2011). Love, hate and indigestion. *Psychoanalytica Obscura*, *92*, 45–6.

Sachertorte, V. (1932). *The wisdom of obesity*. Krankheit Press.

Stücke, J. (2021). Warum werde ich immer zuletzt ausgewählt? *Festschrift für Pete Rose, 17*, 232–56.

The Last Word

Your arrival at this page indicates that you have either finished the book or skipped to the end for the punch line. If the former is the case, thank you for hearing me out. I hope it gave you something to take back to your office.

If you skipped to the end looking for the reveal, here it is in seven bullet points:

- Patients can be described by dozens of diagnostic terms, but not usually in ways that are helpful to the analytic clinician. What I have found useful is attention to the syntax of thought that delineates three different categories of life experience: the repressed oedipal thinking of the neurotic; the wishful, shortsighted thinking of the perverse; and the concrete, disordered thinking of the psychotic.
- Sadism is distinguishable from aggression, to good clinical effect. Sadomasochism is an effort to tie one person to another, whereas aggression seeks to destroy the tie.
- Analytic therapy is hard work because it is an encounter between two people, both governed by forces about which they know very little, engaging each other and their respective demons in an unwelcome, intense, passionate, terrifying dialogue. Theory is often misused in a fruitless effort to make those feelings disappear and to provide distance from the patient.
- Analysis is an oscillation between enacting and reflecting, between joining and separating. The analytic literature is not very good at capturing the intensity of feeling, nor the stumbling, lurching, working in the dark that characterizes much of clinical work.
- Analytic therapy is not a reproducible therapy. Each analyst is unique, each patient is unique, each analytic pair is unique.
- Clinical work correlates poorly with the analyst's theoretical orientation. The character traits of the analyst are better indicators of how that analyst actually works.
- Incomprehensibility is not a hallmark of good analytic writing.

DOI: 10.4324/9781003360391-27

In my discussion of character traits defining analysts, I omitted one important topic: What kind of person becomes an analytic therapist? As an "impossible profession," it is clearly not for everyone. I imagine the motivation to become an analyst must include reparative fantasies for our thought-crimes, fear of our sadism, and, for male-identified therapists, envy of the maternal. However you got here, if you are an experienced therapist, then you know that every therapy expands the analyst as it expands the patient.

And you know that, despite the formidable challenges of the work, it is an astonishing privilege to be granted access to the depths of another soul, to have a hand in the liberation of another heart and mind.

Index